HAND-BUILDING POTTERY

DISCOVER THE 4 SIMPLE & PROVEN TECHNIQUES FOR MAKING QUALITY CERAMICS WITH STEPS ON FORMING, FIRING, AND GLAZING YOUR CLAY FROM START TO FINISH

CHLOE BECKER

CONTENTS

INTRODUCTION

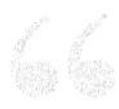 *Pottery is eighty percent technique and only twenty percent art.*

— AH LEON

Do you spend hours perfecting your pottery only to be left with uneven edges and walls? Do you feel frustrated and limited in your ability to improve your skills while others judge your capabilities? I understand the pain you're experiencing. As an experienced ceramicist, you know the value of creating beautiful works that reflect your creativity and passion. But falling short of your goals can be discouraging.

That's why I'm thrilled to introduce this book to you. It's the perfect solution to help you overcome these challenges and take your pottery to the next level. You deserve to feel confident and proud of your creations.

In the world of pottery, there has been a fascinating evolution influenced by different cultures and technological advancements. New tools such as digital pottery wheels to electric kilns and slab rollers have introduced exciting possibilities. Moreover, technology and social media have played a significant role in introducing a new generation to pottery. These platforms have become a vibrant hub for sharing and promoting pottery, inspiring enthusiasts to showcase their work and connect with a broader audience.

Pottery is not just a craft; it's a form of expression that combines cognitive and sensory activities. Its therapeutic benefits are widely recognized, providing a calming and stress-relieving outlet. And it's not limited to any gender. Men and women embrace pottery as a medium for personal growth and creative exploration.

For thousands of years, pottery has captivated artists with its ability to convey visual statements through form and color. Despite the distractions of the digital age, pottery remains timeless and continues to be one of the most sought-after art forms. It allows you to disconnect from technology and immerse yourself fully in the tactile experience of shaping clay. The joy of creating something with your own hands is incomparable.

This book will be your trusted companion, providing you with the knowledge, techniques, and shortcuts you need to make remarkable progress. You'll be amazed at how quickly you'll improve and how your confidence will soar. Imagine the satisfaction of creating beautiful, well-crafted ceramics that truly reflect your artistic vision.

I invite you to keep reading and discover the transformative power of this book. I'm excited to hear how it has helped you unlock your creative potential and witness the incredible progress you'll make. Together, let's embark on a journey of growth and artistic fulfillment!

WHY SHOULD I BUY THIS BOOK?

In this book, you'll find everything you need to refine your pottery-making skills, whether you are a beginner or an experienced potter. It's a must-have resource that will guide you through the intricate pottery-making process and help you achieve remarkable results.

By practicing the techniques outlined in this book, you'll experience a significant boost in your confidence and see a noticeable improvement in your pottery creations. From shaping the clay to firing and glazing, every stage of the process is covered in detail, providing valuable insights and techniques to ensure your success. What sets this book apart is its comprehensive and detailed approach. It offers step-by-step instructions and practical tips that have been carefully curated to help you easily navigate pottery-making challenges. You'll learn the secrets of precision and attention to detail, crucial elements that contribute to creating beautiful and functional pieces.

But this book is more than just a guide for personal improvement. It empowers you to share your knowledge and pass on your skills to others. With the confidence and expertise gained from this book, you can inspire and teach others, creating a ripple effect of creativity and knowledge-sharing within the pottery community. Whether you're ready to embark on your pottery journey or looking to take your craft to the next level, this book is the perfect tool to help you achieve your goals. It provides a solid foundation of knowledge and techniques to enhance your pottery-making skills and unleash your creative potential.

Take advantage of this incredible opportunity to enhance your skills and craft. Invest in yourself and seize the chance to create beautiful, meaningful pottery that embodies your creative vision. Your journey awaits!

1

A LOOK INTO HAND-BUILDING POTTERY

Throughout human history, ceramics have played a crucial role in uncovering the mysteries of our past by providing a glimpse into the lives of our ancestors. Pottery, dating back thousands of years, has helped to date heritage excavations, and shed light on trade connections and artistic styles within societies. From humble beginnings as a storage medium, pottery has grown into a significant industry, encompassing both practical and creative forms.

History of Pottery

In the past, people would transfer water using handwoven baskets. The water, specifically from streams, would contain some sediment. The sediment would form the shape of the basket upon drying. Gradually, individuals became aware that these sediment coatings could be utilized as robust storage items. They collected sediment, molded it, and sun-dried or baked it in hot ashes. As a result, the initial clay containers (and, consequently, all pottery) came into existence.

The Neolithic Age witnessed a sharp rise in the use of ceramics alongside agriculture and farming practiced by settled communities. Clay-based ceramics gained popularity as art pieces, tiles, bricks, and containers for food and liquids. Its use traveled from Asia to the Middle East and Europe.

The ancient Egyptians are commonly acknowledged as the inventors of kilns; they utilized bricks made of clay and straw for insulation. In addition, they were innovators in applying glaze to their pottery before firing. Like its contemporary counterpart, this glaze provided the pottery with a smooth and glossy finish, rendering it impermeable.

Greek vases are a perfect example of pottery evolution, showcasing elaborate paintings depicting their mythology. In the medieval era, people discovered that incorporating sand into the clay made vessels sturdy enough to endure direct exposure to fire. This method also prevented distortion, cracking, or bursting of pieces due to high heat inside the kiln.

In the 13th century, German artisans created stoneware by firing strong clays at high temperatures, making impermeable vessels. Chinese potters developed porcelain by blending feldspar and kaolin, resulting in delicate items. Other potters in Asia and Europe developed techniques to imitate Chinese porcelain. Japanese potters invented kintsugi, an artistic method of repairing broken pottery with gold or silver.

Overall, the development of pottery has been driven by innovation and practicality, resulting in diversity and exquisite beauty that continues to be cherished and appreciated today.

Types of Pottery

Pottery has a rich history and has evolved over the centuries to reach the modern era. Artists use various pottery techniques to create both decorative and functional pieces. Earthenware, stoneware, and porcelain are common types of pottery, each using different clays and clay mixtures that include silica and minerals.

Earthenware pottery made directly from clay without being vitrified at high temperatures. Slip is applied to Earthenware to make it waterproof.

Porcelain, a popular type of clay, is created by combining kaolin clay and china stone and firing it at high temperatures in a kiln. Its white appearance is one of its distinguishing features, while its strength and heat resistance make it a sought-after material.

For this book, the main types of clay we'll focus on are stoneware and earthenware.

Basics of Pottery

To become a skilled potter, there's some basic guidelines that you should follow. You can establish a pottery workshop at home with some effort and a solid foundation in the fundamentals. Start by researching the best kilns for your region. Remember that both gas and electric kilns require unique connections and consumable supplies. Set up a dedicated workspace for your pottery wheel in a well-ventilated area, and ensure you have plenty of level surfaces to work on. With these steps in mind, you'll be well on your way to mastering the art of pottery.

Regarding kiln ovens, you have two options: gas or electric. Both options have distinct features that artists can consider based on their requirements. Electric ovens are more commonly used for convenience and ease of setup but are better suited for low and mid-fire clay. If you're working with high-fire clay, gas ovens are the ideal choice, providing interesting surface textures in earthy hues and better temperature control, though they require special permits.

Various types of clay with different mineral and silica compositions can be used to achieve unique ceramic pottery effects. However, it's essential to be cautious while working with dry clay powder, as it contains silica that can be harmful if inhaled. To protect your lungs, wearing a mask while handling clay is recommended. Using wet clay is a better option to avoid inhaling any harmful particles.

Once the clay has been fired in a bisque state, it's prepped for a glaze coating. This coating provides tensile strength to the ceramic and makes it waterproof. Glazes are typically made from a blend of minerals and silica. When heated, the glaze liquefies and then solidifies again on the surface of the clay. It's important to note that the glazes used must correspond to the firing temperature of the clay.

Hand-Building Pottery

Hand-building is a traditional way of making pottery that involves shaping structures without using a pottery wheel. This method is achieved by using different techniques and simple pottery tools.

Pinch pottery, coil building, slab building, and press mold pottery are the four most prevalent hand-building pottery techniques. Before the invention of the potter's wheel, hand-building was the only technique to make ceramics.

Pinch pottery is a technique where you shape clay by pressing it into a ball with your thumb and shaping it in one hand. You can create various items such as pinch pots, oil lamps, candle holders, smudge pots, incense burners, mortar and pestle sets, and even salt and pepper shakers. It's an excellent way for beginners to start working with clay.

Coiled pottery involves creating long clay coils and then interlocking them to create a more significant piece. You can shape the coils in any form or size you want. Coil pottery offers a range of design possibilities, including patterned coil pots, distinctive coil bowls, smooth coil mugs, woven coil pots, and many other creative forms. You can also combine pinch pottery with coil pottery to make a flat dish as a foundation for coiled pots.

Slab pottery combines flat clay slabs to create various forms, such as plates, cups, and sculptures. A slab roller is used to create flat slabs quickly and easily. You can also use paper templates and slump molds to help you plan and shape your project.

Press mold pottery involves creating a mold by pressing clay onto an object, which leaves a negative impression, or by pressing clay into the mold to make a positive impression in the clay. This technique allows the artist to create functional and decorative pottery replicas, such as soap dishes, drawer pulls, figurines, and textured clay pieces.

Materials and Tools Required for Hand-Building

Before starting the hand-building process, it's essential to have the necessary materials and tools at your disposal. With the right equipment, you can create beautiful and functional pottery pieces. In this section, we will go over the essential items you need for hand-building pottery.

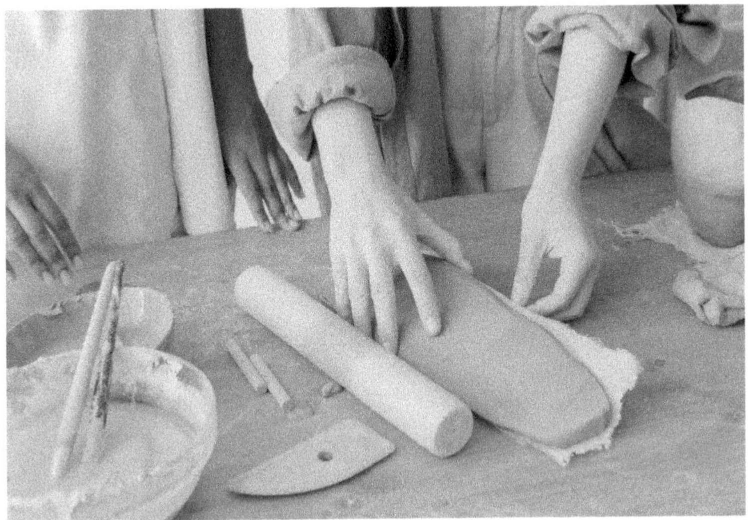

Clay

For hand-building pottery, I recommended using earthenware clay because it is sturdy and malleable. You can store it in a thick plastic bag to retain its moisture. Using pre-made damp clay is a convenient option.

Tools

Pin Tool

A pin tool is helpful for slicing, puncturing, engraving patterns, and piercing small holes in the clay. Several potters prefer to recycle dental instruments, as these have the characteristics to give precise patterns and texture to the piece.

Wire Cutter

Clay wire cutters are tools used for cutting clay during pottery-making and dividing large masses of clay that range from 5 to 50 lbs. This tool is made with a wire stretched between two handles. To use a clay wire cutter, place the wire onto the clay and press down while pulling it toward you, slicing through it. Clay wire cutters are handy for cutting even slices of clay, such as when creating slabs for slab pottery or cutting clay from a larger block for throwing on the wheel. They can also cut excess clay from a piece or trim the base of a pot after removing it from the wheel.

Score Tools

A scoring tool is used in pottery to create textured or decorative designs and combine two clay pieces. It is typically a pointed tool used to scratch the surface of the clay before attaching another piece of clay. This creates tiny grooves and ridges that allow the clay pieces to adhere more securely when pressed together. The score marks provide a rough surface area that helps the slip penetrate and bond the two clay pieces together. The scoring tool is also useful for carving designs and patterns into the clay surface, allowing the artist to create unique and intricate details on their pottery.

Silicone Placemats

Flattening clay slabs evenly requires physical effort; potters can use two canvas sheets and a rolling pin to achieve this. However, some prefer silicone placemats instead of canvas sheets, which helps prevent clay dust.

Slab Roller

A slab roller flattens and shapes clay into uniform slabs for various projects.

Brayer

A brayer is a tool used in pottery to flatten and smooth out clay surfaces. It resembles a rolling pin but has a handle on one end and a hard rubber roller on the other. To use a brayer, the potter places the clay object on a smooth surface, then rolls the brayer back and forth over the clay surface to compress and smooth it. Brayers smooth out slabs, attach clay pieces, and create even textures on clay surfaces.

Templates

Templates create duplicate designs on objects. These are cut out from heavy stock papers. The templates act like patterns for hand-building projects. They also make patterns and designs on the surface of pottery by placing them over the clay and using tools to trace or carve around the edges.

Rubber Rib

Rubber ribs are used in pottery to shape and smooth clay surfaces. They compress and refine the surface of the clay, remove excess water, and create soft curves and edges. They are versatile tools at every stage of the pottery-making process, from shaping and throwing to trimming and glazing.

Spray Bottle

A spray bottle is a helpful tool in pottery for adding moisture to the clay as you work. When working with clay, it can become dry and difficult to manipulate. By spritzing the clay with water from a spray bottle, you can keep it moist and easier to shape. Using a spray bottle with a delicate mist setting is essential to avoid adding too much water to the clay and causing it to become too wet.

Fettling Knife

A fettling knife is a tool used in pottery to trim and remove excess clay from the surface of a pot or sculpture. It is a flat, sharp blade attached to a handle and is typically made of metal or plastic. The fettling knife is also helpful in cutting shapes or patterns into the clay and scoring the clay's surface in preparation for adding handles or other decorative elements.

Sponge

Sponges are a commonly used tool in pottery for shaping, smoothing, and cleaning the surface of clay. Depending on the desired effect, they add or remove moisture from the clay. A damp sponge smooths out a pot's surface or removes excess clay, while a dry sponge creates texture or absorbs water from the surface of the clay. Sponges are also helpful in cleaning pottery tools and work surfaces during pottery-making.

Equipment

Banding Wheel

A banding wheel is a rotating platform used in pottery to help the potter work on their piece from various angles without picking it up. You can use your hands, tools, or brushes to work on the piece while turning the wheel to access different sides of the piece easily. It's also beneficial for decorating, glazing, and trimming the piece's base.

Clay Molds

Molds are used in pottery to help create consistent and repeatable forms. They can be made of a variety of materials, such as plaster, wood, or plastic, and come in different shapes and sizes.

Studio Tip 1: Things You Need to Know About Clay-Making

Whether you are an amateur or a seasoned artist, here are a couple of tips that will enhance your pottery and studio knowledge in multiple ways.

- **Proper posture matters**: Before starting the wedging process, it's crucial to ensure proper posture and correct setup of your wedging table. As wedging will be a regular part of your pottery practice, finding the appropriate posture and table height is essential for comfortable and practical wedging. If you experience discomfort in your back, your table might be too low, while pressure on your arms or shoulders could indicate that your table is too high. Therefore, maintaining the correct posture and table height is crucial for a successful pottery experience.
- **Work on a proper surface**: Choosing a suitable surface to work on is important to ensure a non-sticky working surface for clay. Convenient options for wedging clay

include granite, Masonite, and concrete surfaces. Plywood, plywood covered in fabric, and plaster are also common alternatives.

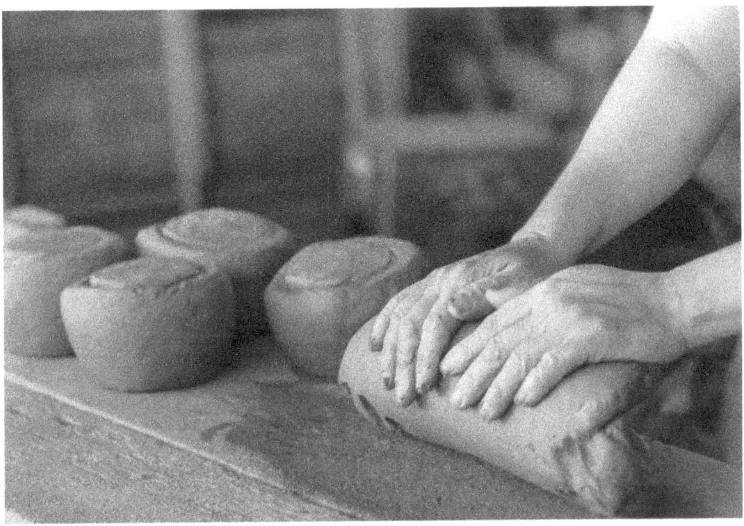

Carefully select which material you'll use to cover your pottery workspace with. While fabric placemats or canvas may seem like a good option, they can attract and trap clay dust that contains silica. Inhaling too much silica dust can lead to silicosis, a disease that makes breathing difficult. To stay safe, consider using alternative materials that don't trap dust, cleaning your workspace after every session, and wearing a mask while around clay dust. While using clay is generally safe with proper precautions, consider an alternative to avoid constantly washing canvas mats. Nonporous, wipeable surfaces like silicone placemats are a great option, and wearing a mask when working with clay is a healthy choice.

- **Weigh the clay:** It is an excellent habit to weigh the clay that the project requires. If you are a beginner, start with a piece weighing 2 to 3 pounds.
- **Wet-wipe surfaces:** After working with clay, it is essential to clean the area thoroughly. However, it's important to note that sweeping or vacuuming can put dust back into the air. Instead, opt for wet wiping using cleaning wipes or microfiber wash rags, which can be washed and reused. If

there is clay dust on the floor, it is best to mop or sprinkle the floor with water and use a commercial-sized squeegee for clean-up. This will ensure a more effective and safer clean-up.

- **Recycle clay**: Recycling clay is possible and appropriate for ceramicists who want to learn an additional skill. It involves getting familiar with the dry clay and clay soil and thoroughly understanding the refining and priming stages required to render it usable. Please remember that this process can only be done with dried-out clay that has yet to be fired.

Studio Tip 2: Essentials in your Pottery Studio to Get Started

A pottery studio needs a few basic supplies to make the art form practical. Seasoned artists will acknowledge several of these important components:

- Keep the **apron** handy to keep your clothes tidy and free from messes while working with clay.
- It is even better to keep **messy clothes** in your studio that you use as your working uniform.
- **Plasterboards** are great tools for wedging clay. These are also used to recycle clay and to dry the pieces thrown out of the wheel.
- **Plastic buckets** are indispensable, some have lids, and some don't. The ones with lids are used for glazes, while the ones without lids are used to gather dry clay fragments or for throwing water. A couple of rectangular buckets are usually set up to prevent the clay from drying out once it has been opened.
- **Shelves** are plentiful. These are great for storing pieces. There should be enough room to separate refined products from ceramics that need to be bisque-fired or glazed. Shelves help to keep the studio organized.
- **Plastic bags** are ideal for covering small items like cups, and large sheets of thick plastic can cover large quantities of ceramic.

- **Canvas sheets** are used while flattening the clay and air-dry clay slabs. They are composed of dense fabric and remain stable while the clay is rolled out. It also absorbs a substantial amount of moisture from the clay but not an excessive amount.
- In the studio, **wooden boards** are beneficial for maneuvering newly thrown objects or curing clay slabs.
- A **wheel bat system** is one of the most efficient ways to throw on the wheels. The fact that you can return to your piece later and make changes or add finishing touches while it is still firmly attached to the bat is a significant reason to own one.
- A **Giffin Grip** is a re-centering tool that is handy for various uses. Your leather-hard parts can be easily trimmed. Giffin Grip can also help with the glazing process and waxing bottoms.
- A wide range of **molds** for texture, design, small and big shapes is a must-have in the pottery studio.
- Wearing a **dust mask** when working on a project in a small space where you spray glazes or handle clay particles is recommended. The majority of glazes include alumina, which is airborne. While combining powdered glazes, it's a good practice to put on a dust mask.

You will require clay, a kiln, hand tools, and a suitable workspace to create your own pottery. Clay is one of the prerequisites to begin pottery making. Several varieties of pottery clay differ because most clays contain many clay minerals and varying concentrations of metal oxides and organic materials. Clay can be categorized into multiple groups depending on its attributes and the temperature required to mature or attain its maximum strength and resilience. The following chapter will acquaint you with everything you should know about clay.

2

ALL ABOUT THE CLAY

Pottery-making involves four main stages. First, the soft clay is shaped into the desired form. Then, the piece goes through the drying stage, where any remaining moisture evaporates, making it ready for the next step. In the third stage, the piece is solidified through firing methods. Finally, decorative colors and water-resistant sealing are applied in the glazing stage before the last firing. Understanding different clay properties is essential for mastering the craft. We will go over six distinct clay phases within these four main stages.

The Different Stages of Clay

Clay exhibits distinct characteristics during the various phases of its drying and firing process. Understanding these stages is crucial for successful pottery-making. Here are the six critical phases involved in working with clay:

Slip Clay

Slip clay is a semi-liquid mixture of clay and water used as decoration or a bonding agent for combining clay pieces. It ensures a strong connection when fired. Slip also makes molds, typically achieved by mixing it with a 50/50 combination of water and a deflocculant like Darvan or Sodium silicate. These additives create a more fluid consistency, which is beneficial for slip casting. Slip casting involves pouring slip into a plaster mold to create pottery forms.

Tip for Slip: You may create the best slip from your clay. Remember that slip works best when it has sour cream consistency when decorating or joining clay pieces.

Wet Clay (Malleable Stage)

Wet clay is the state of clay that is fresh and newly prepared, containing the highest moisture content. It's highly malleable and can be easily shaped and manipulated.

Leather-hard Clay

As the clay begins to lose moisture, it enters the leather-hard stage. At this point, the clay retains its shape while remaining slightly malleable. It can be trimmed, carved, and refined with tools. Leather-hard clay is ideal for adding intricate details and textures.

Bone-Dry Stage of Clay

The drying phase is completed when all the moisture has evaporated from the clay, indicating it is ready for bisque firing. It is incredibly fragile and delicate, making it prone to breakage. It is crucial to handle bone-dry clay with care before firing. Drying may require a minimum of seven days or more, depending on the weather conditions in your region and the size of the art piece. Attaining the bone-dry phase of your clay is of utmost significance to ensure a successful firing.

Bisque Stage of Clay

The first firing prepares the clay for glazing by altering its malleable state to a hardened ceramic form while remaining sufficiently porous to absorb glazes.

Glaze Firing Stage of Clay

The final stage involves glazing the bisque-fired clay. Glaze is a mixture of minerals and pigments that, when applied to the surface, forms a glass-like coating when fired again. Glazing adds decorative colors, texture, and water-resistant sealing to the pottery piece. The glaze firing brings out vibrant colors and creates a durable finish.

Choosing The Clay

Type of Clay

For newcomers, the most recommended clay bodies are earthenware and stoneware. Consider a few factors before choosing your clay: the type, color, strength, plasticity, texture, price and availability within your region, firing temperatures, and cone sizes. While selecting your clay, you must be aware of a few factors.

Earthenware is an excellent option for hand-building pottery due to its high plasticity and ability to retain shape. Its porosity makes it suitable for making outdoor building materials like bricks and flowerpots, as it can withstand freezing temperatures without cracking. However, finished earthenware pieces are prone to chipping and cracking compared to stoneware, so it is important to build with thicker layers. The hues of earthenware primarily range from red, orange to buff-white, and additional granules or sand can enhance texture and strength.

Stoneware is preferred for dinnerware and mugs due to its strength and resistance to chipping compared to earthenware. It contains naturally occurring grog, enhancing its flexibility during forming. With varying amounts of sand or grog added to the clay, artists can create a wide range of forms with stoneware. It is available in hues such as white, buff, brown, and various shades of grey.

When choosing your clay, it's essential to know whether it contains either grog or sand or neither.

Clay Strength

When it comes to clay strength, this is crucial in pottery and ceramics for several reasons. It directly impacts the structural integrity of pottery pieces, preventing cracking and warping. Strong clay allows for easier shaping and manipulation, enabling intricate detailing and precise carving. It supports complex forms, ensuring they maintain shape during drying and firing. Additionally, clay strength will influence firing behavior and aid you in selecting the appropriate techniques and temperatures.

Cone Size—What Are Cones Used For?

In pottery, cones play a vital role in representing the kiln's firing or maximum temperature. When cones are placed inside the kiln during firing, they help potters determine if their pieces have been fired correctly. Understanding cones and converting their measurements to Fahrenheit or Celsius is crucial to avoid costly mistakes.

The cone size is essential when selecting clay, as different clay types have varying firing temperatures. It's necessary to match the cone size of your clay with the glaze firing stage, as clay and glaze undergo expansion and contraction together. By being mindful of the kiln's firing temperature and considering the cone size of your clay body and glaze when purchasing clay, you can ensure compatibility and achieve successful firings. This helps prevent differential expansion and contraction issues, leading to optimal results in pottery-making.

Low-fire

The low-fire zone ranges between Cone 022 (1087 °F or 586 °C) to Cone 2 (2088 °F or 1142 °C). The most frequently used range in the low fire category is Cone 04 to Cone 06. Generally, earthenware is a low-fire clay, mostly bisque-fired with cone 4 and glaze-fired at Cones 5 or 6. Earthenware should never be fired at higher temperatures than this because it will start melting.

Mid-fire

The mid-fire range varies from Cone 3 (1152 °C or 2106 °F) to Cone 7 (1239 °C or 2262 °F); frequently used ones are Cone 5 and Cone 6.

Mid-range firing is favored because of the abundant available glaze hues and its suitability for dinnerware. Stoneware is commonly fired at two different temperatures: the mid-fire range, which is widely between Cones 5 and 6, and the high-fire range, which is often Cone 10.

High-fire

Cone 8 (1249 °C to 2280 °F) to Cone 10 (1285 °C to 2345 °F) fall in the category of high-fire, and the most widely used is Cone 10.

When purchasing clay, ensure the label specifies the cone size for firing. If the information needs to be included, avoid buying such clay, as you won't know the appropriate firing temperature. When selecting a cone size, avoid those with a leading zero. Keep in mind that low-firing glazes or clay may melt in the kiln.

Price of Clay

When starting pottery, consider checking the availability of earthenware and stoneware in your region to ensure reasonable pricing, helping you make an informed choice. Recycling clay can be a great option if you are passionate about nature and sustainability.

Best Clay for Hand-Building Pottery

When it comes to hand-building pottery, the best clay option is earthenware. It's sticky, making it popular among hand-building potters and effectively retaining molded shapes. To enhance its properties, choosing an earthenware clay brand with some grog or sand additions is beneficial, especially for creating the beautiful red hue of terracotta.

While stoneware can be used for functional pottery, earthenware remains the top choice for hand-building techniques due to its plasticity and the ability to maintain its shape once molded. Earthenware clay is beneficial if you're new to pottery and taking time.

3

FORMING CLAY

I n this chapter, we will explore the various aspects of forming clay. We'll debunk the myth surrounding air bubbles, discuss different wedging clay styles, explain why wedging is essential, and delve into various methods of shaping clay, including the bonding pinch, pushing out, and flat pinch. Let's dive in and discover the fascinating world of clay formation.

Pottery explosions inside the kiln are distressing. Many believe that air pockets in clay cause these explosions, but that's not entirely true. The moisture trapped within air pockets leads to explosions, as the clay hasn't dried properly. The kiln's rising temperature causes the moisture to evaporate rapidly, turning into steam. The pressure from the expanding steam causes the clay to burst. Therefore, the clay must be completely dry before firing. Even without air bubbles, explosions can occur if the clay isn't thoroughly dried.

Wedging Clay

Before starting pottery production, the clay piece goes through a preparation stage called wedging. Wedging is a process that helps make the slightly sticky clay smoother and easier to work with, which is essential for shaping it effectively. When the clay is freshly taken out of the bag, wedging it at least 30 times is recommended. However, if you have recycled clay, you should knead it at least 100 times or more, depending on the condition of the clay. In this next section, you will learn about the different techniques for wedging clay.

The Ram's Head

The ram's head wedging style prepares the clay for pottery. It involves a specific hand motion that resembles the shape of a ram's head. To perform the ram's head wedging technique, you can follow these instructions to prepare your clay:

- Start by cutting your clay into two equal parts.
- Place the clay sections side-by-side on a wedging table or work surface.
- Position both hands on the clay, with your palms pressing down.
- Apply downward pressure with your hands while rotating the clay in a circular motion simultaneously. Ensure to push the clay in and do not fold over.
- Continue kneading and folding the clay, maintaining the circular motion with your hands; this motion ensures that the clay particles mix thoroughly, eliminating air pockets and achieving a more consistent texture.
- As you work the clay, you'll notice a spiral pattern forming, resembling the horns of a ram.
- Keep kneading and rotating the clay until the spiral pattern becomes more pronounced.
- Once you have completely worked your clay, shape it into a circular form by rolling the end and softly pushing the sides. Finally, mold it into a ball.

Now, press downwards and inwards. Make sure to push the ram's horn inward by at least an eighth of an inch with the pads of your hands just below your thumbs as you press down and away. Begin a rocking action while pressing in, down, and out and dragging the clay back toward you.

Using the ram's head wedging style with these steps will help improve the consistency and malleability of your clay.

The Spiral

The spiral or shell wedging style with clay is simple to learn. This technique produces a swirl design similar to the ram's head approach. The spiral thoroughly mixes the clay by eliminating any lumps, making the clay more workable and successfully removing air bubbles. Remember that while wedging with this method, you merely press down with a twist. If you are doing it right, your clay will have a spiral form that resembles a shell, which you can see fairly quickly. Here's a step-by-step explanation of how to perform this wedging style:

- Start with a lump of clay and place it on a clean surface, such as a wedging table.
- Use the heel of your hand to press down on the clay, creating a flat, circular shape.
- Begin at the outer edge of the clay circle and apply pressure while moving your hand in a spiral motion toward the center.
- As you continue this spiral motion, gradually push the clay forward with your palm while keeping the pressure consistent.
- Repeat this spiral motion, moving from the outer edge toward the center while gradually pushing the clay forward.
- After several rotations, you will notice that the clay starts to form a spiral shape or resemble a shell.
- Continue this spiral or shell wedging motion until the clay becomes smooth, homogenous, and free from air bubbles.
- Once you have achieved the desired texture, the clay can be shaped and molded into your desired pottery form.

The spiral or shell wedging style is an effective technique for properly mixing clay particles and eliminating any air pockets. It helps create a consistent clay texture, making it easier to work with during pottery creation.

The Stack and Slam

This technique is one of the simplest and most effective ways to compress clay, which helps to minimize cracking. Begin with the rectangular-shaped clay, then slice it into two halves with the wire's help. As though folding it over, stack the clay on top of one another. Remember not to dig your fingers into the clay, which can create air bubbles in the piece. Keep the clay on the wedging board. To compress the clay together, continue rotating it into a rectangular shape and beat it down five to seven times.

Once you have finished manipulating the clay, it will be rectangular. To ensure the moisture content is evenly distributed throughout the clay, you should slam the corners down to create a ball. Your clay is ready to use now.

This is the simplest way for wedging clay and is ideal for potters with wrist issues.

Why Is It Important to Wedge the Clay?

Here are a couple of reasons that make wedging an essential task for potters.

- Clay has lumps, and if you wish to have a smooth pottery experience, you will have to wedge your clay to get rid of the large lumps.
- Wedging makes the clay plastic, and when the clay becomes flexible, it is easier to mold.
- In ceramics, homogeneous clay means evenly distributing moisture throughout your clay. As your pottery will cure more uniformly if your clay is consistent, you can lessen the chance it will break.
- Air bubbles are a nuisance for potters, and wedging helps eliminate air bubbles.

The ram's head wedge and the spiral wedge methods wedge the clay by combining it in a circular motion. Wedging is practical and straightforward, and the stack and slam technique is the simplest.

Formation Approaches for Clay

Hand-building clay has unbeatable beauty, and potters who create designs by hand must master the skill by learning the different forming techniques of clay.

Bonding Pinch

The Bonding Pinch method simplifies the process of hand-building pottery. By utilizing this technique, you can easily connect clay coils to the base of your pottery. It is crucial to ensure a secure meshing of the bonding pinch to establish a sturdy foundation.

Apply pressure using your index finger to achieve a strong bond between the coil and the base. This pressure helps firmly join the coil to the base, ensuring the piece maintains its structural stability throughout the pottery-making process.

Pushing Out

The Pushing Out method offers a perfect opportunity to shape your pottery piece according to your desired form or make necessary alterations. This technique relies heavily on your creativity, allowing you to use your hands or tools to achieve the desired shape.

Success with this technique hinges on understanding the appropriate pressure, hand movements, and clay thickness required. These factors play a vital role in achieving the desired outcome. The Pushing Out method is particularly effective for creating ceramics with a broader appearance, as they allow for easy manipulation of the clay from the inside out using your fingers.

Flat Pinch

The Flat Pinch method allows you to shape the ceramic using your thumb and forefingers. This technique is beneficial for creating pieces with a thinner profile. To enhance maneuverability, utilize your non-dominant hand to gently run through the clay, resulting in a smoother texture.

Applying pressure with your fingers is key to achieving the desired thinness in the clay. This technique is especially effective for creating pieces with a thicker base that gradually thins out toward the top.

In summary, this chapter has comprehensively explored the various aspects of forming clay. We have dispelled the myth surrounding air bubbles, examined different wedging clay styles, and highlighted the significance of wedging in the pottery process. Additionally, we have delved into a range of methods for shaping clay. In the next chapter, we will delve into the intricacies of hand-forming clay, unlocking a realm of artistic expression and exploration.

4

PINCH POTTERY

Pinch pottery is a simple yet creative technique within ceramics that requires only enthusiasm and skill to master. This chapter explores forming clay into unique vessels, crafting bases, and adding distinctive features such as spouts and brims. Although it may seem basic, pinch pottery allows for limitless artistic expression.

Pinch Pots

Pinch pots are hand-formed, little, circular clay pots. Pinch pottery involves gently pinching outward from the center of the clay ball to produce a bowl or vase. Pinch pots can be quickly assembled and decorated using several processes, including painting, carving, decals, enamels, and glazing.

Your thumb is pivotal because it is used as a dominant player to press the clay into the center. Use the other hand to cup the ball by pinching the center of the clay with your fingers and thumb. Rotate the ball using the other hand, pinching on the sides.

Put the clay ball on a newspaper or thin board, gently rotating it while carefully pinching it into the appropriate form.

And, if you notice a small hole or tear in the piece during the process, you can easily fill it with a bit of extra clay.

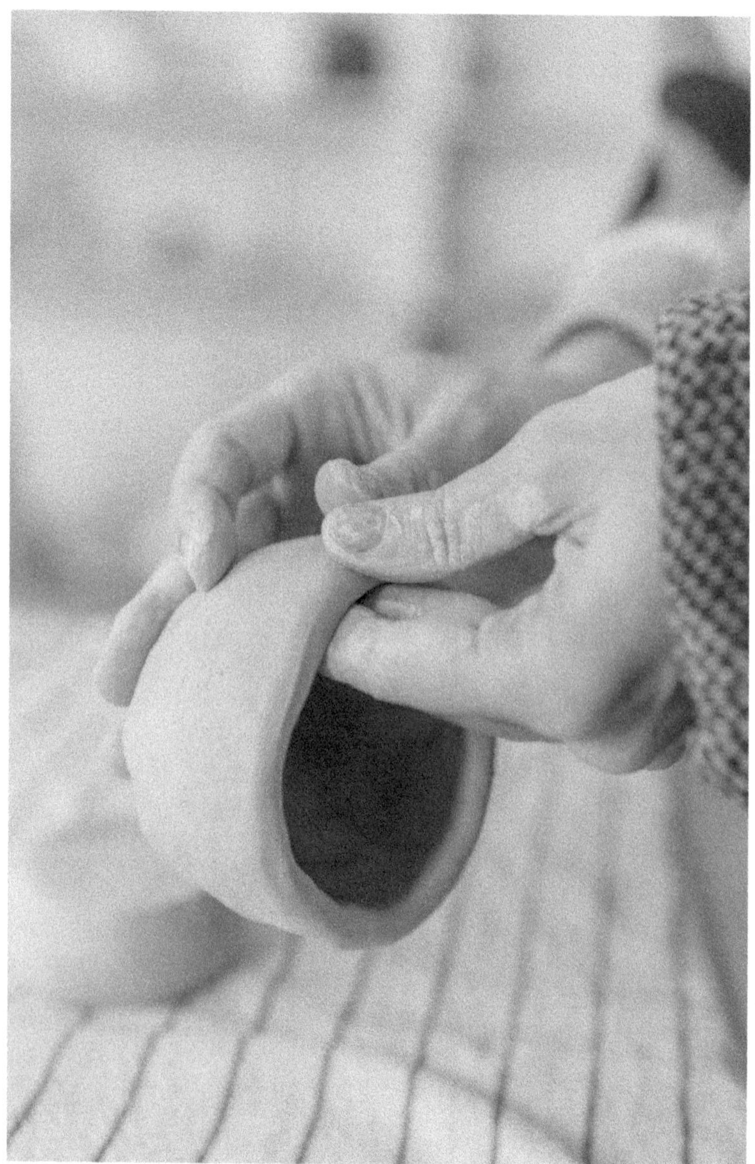

Challenges Faced with Pinch Pottery

Undoubtedly, pinch pottery is the easiest way to learn pottery and usually the first technique covered in beginner's lessons. There are a few common challenges that many beginners encounter during the process of pinch pottery:

- The walls of the pot are uneven.

Beginner potters new to pinch pottery often concentrate on the top portion, unintentionally neglecting the bottom. The concept revolves around working on all sides, starting from the top and extending down to the bottom. It's vital to ensure an even pinching technique on all sides, from the topmost point to the lowest, to achieve a uniform look for the piece.

To make the pot's walls thinner, gently squeeze them, working in around the pot. Continue pinching until the walls reach the desired thickness. The pot's walls should have an equal thickness.

- The rim of the piece may appear thinner.

While pinching the piece, the potter may make the rim thinner than the body and the base. To help with this, turning the pot upside down and carefully lowering it onto a flat surface is one way to level the rim. The pot's outside edges and rim can be smoothed off with a scraper or a curved spoon.

- The form is uneven.

When the piece is being pushed out from the inside, potters must apply a significant amount of pressure with their thumbs throughout the process. Any uneven pressure could result in variations in form, preventing the desired outcome from being achieved. So, applying the same amount of pressure throughout this process is essential.

Pinch Pottery: A Fundamental Pottery Technique

Though pinch pottery is one of the basic techniques to learn pottery without sophisticated tools, it can produce excellent results. Your creativity and imagination are the only constraints to such a skilled form of pottery. You can make anything with these basic pinch pottery techniques:

1. Create a base

Creating a flat base for your pinch pottery is a common phenomenon. Making a curved base will give a unique look to your piece. It is easy to make a curved base. You can take a ball of clay—a plum-sized ball is good enough. Press your thumb into the center of it, leaving approximately half an inch of clay between your thumb and the outer wall to create a curved bottom. After pressing your thumb into the clay to get the right thickness, carefully rotate the ball anti-clockwise at small intervals of .25 inches, working your way out to the edges until each region has the same thickness.

2. Make a coil and pinch

Simple pinching cannot help to create a complete piece. To give height to your piece, you must make coils with your section of clay. Start shaping the coil while wedging the clay to create lovely, circular coils. Start wedging the clay first, then gradually shift to rolling to make a thick log-like shape with a diameter of approximately 3 inches. Keep compressing the clay, reducing the log size to 2 inches. Ensure the thickness is consistent, then gently roll the coil out with your entire hand.

Apply uniform pressure to the coil's surface gently but firmly, sliding your hands over it from the center to the ends while keeping your hands as flat and relaxed as you can. Ensure your coils are always thick enough; they should always be slightly larger than the desired wall thickness for your task. If, at any point, you think that the coil is uneven, you may reshape it again. You will remove some clay while fastening the coil and building height. To create the desired wall, use a coil approximately 1.5 inches high and .25 inches thick.

3. Secure attachments

You can put your pinched base on the banding wheel. You must score the base heavily and then layer it with slip. Now, rescore the slip-coated base. Place a coil on the slip and cut at a 45-degree angle on either end. Push the ends together and blend them using a round or straight-edged wooden rib while rotating the vessel and working on the sides.

4. Layer addition to create forms

Patience is a vice that will aid in achieving perfection in pinch pottery. Since it takes several days to finish large pieces, working simultaneously on multiple pieces is better. An important thing to note here is that the piece should be slightly softer than leather-hard to facilitate the addition of coils. Depending on the humidity, temperature, sunshine, air movement, and humidity in your workspace, this might take three hours to an entire day.

It will be challenging to manage the form if you attempt to add a coil too soon since the bottom cannot withstand the weight and pressure of the additional coil. The clay will become too dry to mold if you wait too long. Before adding more coils, ensure the base has even levels of moisture. Trim off a little layer of clay to balance the pot before adding more coils. Doing so removes the vessel section that is usually dryer than the remainder, leaving a somewhat more pliable region to add a coil. In this manner, the vessel's height will increase at the same rate.

To join coils in pinch pottery:

   i. Begin by applying a layer of slip and scoring it with a serrated rib along the exposed edge.
  ii. When attaching the coil to the upper layer, use your thumb in an X motion to pinch and add height before placing the coil on top.
 iii. If you need to level the pot before adding a new coil, use an Exacto knife to trim the excess.

Repeat these steps once more.

5. Make handles

Making handles is like creating coils in pinch pottery. The handle's size depends upon the thickness of the piece to which it will be attached. Different size cups and pitchers require different thicknesses of handles. Make the coil with a diameter of about 1 inch for a tall- or medium-sized pitcher. Beginning at the coil's bottom, squeeze upward to create a spine that runs vertically through the coil. To flatten the coil, place it between your thumb and forefinger.

Cutting the coil's ends at a 45-degree angle will make them easier to attach later. Thicken the ends by tapping them. Check the measurement and cut the handle accurately while placing it up to the vessel. When it is sufficiently dried, bend it into the necessary curvature and place it on a table so that you may attach it later without damaging its shape.

6. Make a spout

Roll out a short coil with tapered ends to form a spout. Place the coil on the slipped region after scoring and slipping the area where it will be connected. Carve a gentle arch into the lip when the coil is attached. Carve a gentle arch into the lip as soon as the coil is attached. Cut the lip to the proper height using an Exacto knife, then smooth and shape it with your fingertips to make a curve.

7. Add the finishing touches

Place a ruler over the top of the pitcher so that one edge bisects the spout and sits on the opposing rim before attaching the handle—Mark the area on the pitcher's rim where you will score the handle's attachment points. Retrim the bottom of the handle and secure it, ensuring that the handle's arc and length are appropriate. Once finished, cover the piece with plastic for drying for at least three days. Then, gradually remove the plastic to let the item dry entirely.

Pinch Pottery Projects

The versatility of pinch pottery attracts beginners who are eager to learn and master the craft. Here are a few pinch pot projects that are ideal for beginners.

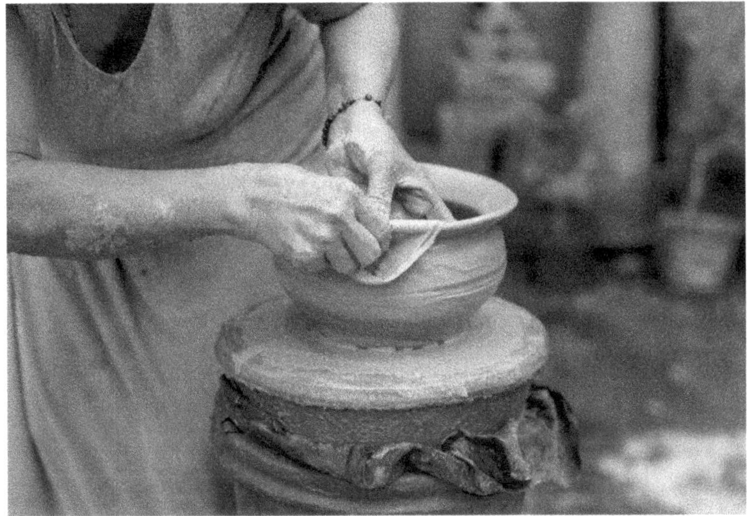

The Thumb Pot

Thumb pots can be as big as a cup or mug but are typically the size of a kiwi fruit. These little pots are best stored in a dry place. Usually located in a culinary space, these miniature containers' uses are conventional for cultivating seeds until the sapling is ready for moving to a more fitting-sized container.

Serving Ware

Unique and exquisite serving ware pieces on the dining table can speak volumes about your knowledge and expertise in pottery. It can serve as an excellent salad bowl or platter to enlighten the dining space and impress your guests. Alternatively, such pieces can adorn the center of your table. You can get creative with your imagination and make the area more attractive by placing dried flowers around or candles to give a formal touch.

Beads

Pinch pottery is one of the most versatile mediums to try your hand at jewelry-making. Crafting your own beads to customize accessories or as materials for your beading pursuit can be a fulfilling artistic and financial undertaking.

Ceramic Pets

Little animal characters made of clay can be an excellent embellishment for your shelves. They look cute and are a great gift for all age groups. Such small items can liven up any space and make you smile. Ceramic animal figurines have been popular for centuries, and recent years have witnessed a fantastic trend of using such items as planters.

Cups and Mugs

Creating mugs or cups with pinch pottery is the most popular. They look cute, quirky, and highly functional. Several professional potters have mastered the art and created their own financial standing by selling their exceptional pieces. You can design your mugs in any height, width, or shape you desire, create a handle that perfectly fits your hand, and decorate them with hues that you or your intended recipients will unquestionably love.

How Can You Perfect Your Pinch Pot Skills?

The most impressive side of pinch pottery is that it does not limit your creativity. If at any point you are dissatisfied with your design, you have the leverage to disintegrate and recreate a new design. You can add more clay and redesign it to satisfy your imagination. However, here are a few tips and tricks to help you acquire the required perfection to excel in pinch pottery.

- *Use different shapes and sizes*

The beauty of pinch pottery allows you to shape it into whatever interests you. If you desire to craft a small embellishment, you can add clay to the pinch pot to modify its size.

- *Create texture on the piece with simple tools*

For a greater aesthetic appeal, some pinch pottery designs incorporate patterns to the surface of the clay. You can create rich textured effects using the most straightforward tools. For example, you can design your piece using a fork. You may also add interest and uniqueness by combining and kneading different-colored clays. Adding sand, gravel, or kneading little fibers into the clay can make it rustic.

- *Handle unfired pots with care before transporting*

If you need to move your pottery items to a kiln situated away from your pottery workplace, put them cautiously in a sturdy, level cardboard box or plastic container, and wrap them with gentle cushioning materials to prevent any displacement or rubbing against one another.

- *Give a perfect finesse by polishing the piece after firing*

Once you have fired your pinch pot, you may refine it by polishing it to attain a refined and expert appearance. Add a small quantity of oil and rotate the pot while wiping it with a cloth. This is a simple and efficient approach to highlighting the inherent attractiveness of your pinch pot. It's crucial to employ a gentle cloth and avoid applying excessive pressure to prevent blemishing the pot.

As we conclude our exploration of pinch pottery, we now embark on another captivating hand-building technique: coil pottery. Coiling involves the art of stacking and merging clay coils to create unique vessels. The following chapter will dive deep into this technique, unraveling the intricacies of building with coils.

5

COIL POTTERY

The coiling method has been widely employed for producing early pottery. Coil pots from early history have been discovered all over the world. Several methods presently utilized to make coil pots can be traced back to ancient times.

What Is Coil Pottery?

Coil pottery is a technique of constructing pottery by hand, in which a potter shapes a foundation, sides, and designs by merging clay coils. The potter twists the clay into coils, arranges them in a pile, and fuses them by exerting pressure to produce a container. The technique of coiled pottery represented a significant advancement in the field of ceramics for our ancient ancestors. When creating large vessels, coil pots proved to be much more robust than either pinch pots or slab-built pots of comparable size. Before throwing wheels, coiling was considered the most effective approach for producing a stable and sizable container.

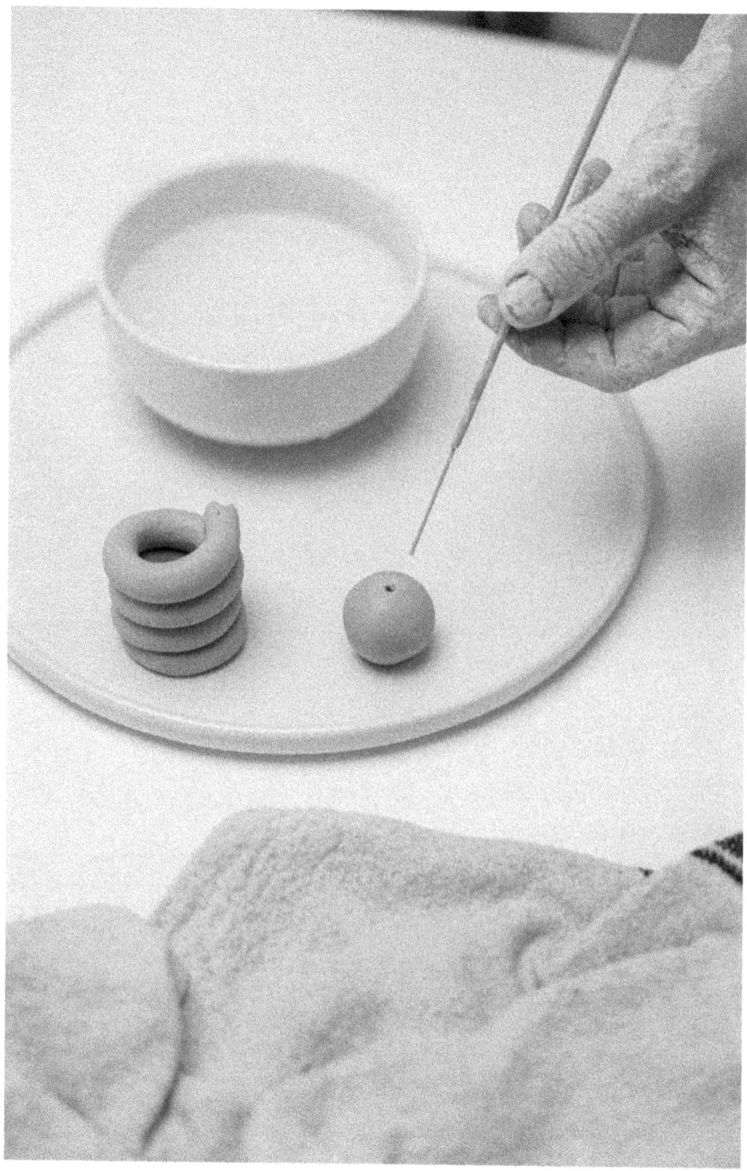

Coil Pottery Technique

Basic coiling techniques make creating attractive and durable pots with unique qualities and distinctiveness possible. It is significant to understand the method of making coil pots.

How can you Make a Coil Pot?

Coiling sessions will be exciting if you incorporate a few tips while making the coil pots.

Making Clay Coils

You may find a few things that could be improved while making clay coils. It is common to encounter challenges like non-uniformity of coil thickness or coil falling flat upon rolling. If you want your coil pot to look attractive, it should be even on all sides.

Here is a simple method to roll clay evenly:

1. Spray a little water on the surface (board) on which you will make a clay coil and allow the board to absorb the water. Wipe out any excess water on the board.
2. Ideally, take a lemon-sized clay ball (the ball should be soft and moist) and squeeze it to make the shape of a sausage using the palm of your hands.
3. Then start rolling the clay on the table, ensuring that you roll it from your fingers to the wrist.
4. Keep twisting the clay ends regularly to not appear flat on any side. This helps maintain the clay piece's uniformity while rolling on the board.
5. Give the desired thinness to the coil.
6. Wrap the coil in a plastic sheet to maintain its texture and prevent it from drying. You can store it in this way for later use. You may continue to make another coil.

Make a batch of coils

Follow the steps mentioned above to make a batch of coils to start your coil pottery without stopping in between to make coils. Moreover, keep wrapping the coils in a plastic sheet, and it will prevent them from drying.

Width of the coil

The width of your coils is determined by the size of what you are constructing. A huge coil pot needs larger coils. However, if you're building a medium-sized bowl or vase, coils approximately the width of your pinky finger are great.

Determine the type of clay required for the project

Good clay for coil pottery should be plastic and robust. Strong clay can sustain its weight during the shaping process. Generally, durable clay comprises some grog, a solid and gritty substance mixed with clay to give it strength.

Your clay should be soft and moist but not greasy and wet. Rolling a coil and looking for two things is a good test. If the coil sticks to the board, it is wet and too soft. You'll know that it's too dry if it develops cracks while being rolled on the board's surface.

Working in stages

If you create a coil pot without a mold, add fewer coils in one go. It will sag if you keep adding weight to the pot in one session. After adding 4–5 coils, allow the pot to sit for 24 hours. You will know it's time to end the session when you feel the pot is becoming too heavy. Setting aside the project and taking a break will give it time to dry and settle into its form.

Methods of Coil Pottery

Now that we've gone through a few tips for making clay coils let's get into the different methods of making coil pottery.

Method #1: Simple Coil Pots

Simple coil pots are constructed by stacking clay coils in sequential rings on top of one another. You may add more complex coil designs, which we will cover later in this chapter. The basic coil pot design comprises simple coils joined together to give a layered coil effect. You can be creative by adding a design to your coil pot.

Let's go over how to make a collared-style coil clay pot.

1. Flatten a piece of clay to form the base of your pot. The base must have the exact thickness of the walls formed by the coil. If the coil is the same width as your little finger, the foundation should be approximately 2/3 inches thick.
2. After you've rolled out your slab, carve out your foundation using a knife or needle tool. If you make a circular pot, score around it with a round item like a lid. This produces a beautiful exact outline to begin constructing.
3. Your base is ready, and you are in a position to start adding coils to your piece. The clay coils must be affixed firmly to the base and each other. If the coils are pressed against each other without a secure attachment, they will shrink and separate while drying or baking. There are two methods you can use to ensure that the coils stick firmly to the base and as a whole:

   a. *Slip and score*

The first method is to slip and score the surface before sticking the coils to one another. First, create a texture on the clay surface to slide and score your surfaces with a modeling tool. A serrated needle tool, fork, or metal tool will suffice. Score the two surfaces you want to unite to make them both rough.

Apply clay slip on the scored surfaces to adhere to the coils. If your clay is moist, you only need to spray a little water on the edges to create slip so the pieces can easily adhere.

Now, you can press both surfaces and squeeze gently. Do not apply harsh pressure while squeezing, as the stress may disturb the shape of the coil. The slip will act as glue to stick the scored surfaces together.

It is necessary to trim the coil to get an even-sized coil. This can be done by placing the coil on or underneath the base and cutting the excess. Use a needle tool or knife to cut the clay. After cutting the coil, bond the edges together with the slip-and-score method.

b. *Blending the coils*

Another method to prevent the clay coils from coming apart during the drying process is to blend the surface of the clay. After positioning the coil, use a modeling tool or thumb to blend the clay coils.

It's important to be mindful of how you handle the pot's surface to maintain the coil pattern's prominence. If you want the coils to be visible mainly on the exterior, it's best to smooth and blend the interior surface of the pot. However, blend the coils very lightly if you aim to showcase the spirals inside and outside. In such cases, carefully slip and score underneath and on top of the coil stacks to ensure they stay securely attached.

When crafting a vase or container meant for holding liquids, it is essential to smooth the interior surface. After applying a glaze to the smooth surface, it becomes wholly sealed and functions well as a vessel.

4. After the slip and score or blending method, you can start constructing the sides of the pot. This is done by adding coils on top of one another using the same procedure.

- Start by cutting your coil to the desired length and securing it using the slip-and-score method for precise results. If you prefer a polished interior surface and enhanced durability for your container, carefully smooth it from the inside.
- If the connections are layered on each other, it can create a vulnerable area on the pot. So, placing the coil joins at different positions on the pot is best. Expanding the circumference of your pot can be achieved by extending the coils slightly toward the outer part of the respective coil, thereby enlarging the walls. Placing your spirals at the inner rim of the underlying spiral will reduce the circumference of your container. In this manner, you may change the size of your container and make it look fascinating.

5. Once you are satisfied with the desired shape of your pot, you can work your way up and keep adding coils.

Method #2: Patterned Coil Pots

This method will familiarize you with making patterned coil clay pots. In this technique, the potter can make different designs on the outer surface or the exterior of the coil pots. Creativity can be at your best while doing this crafty technique. So, let's understand how such pots are made.

1. Start with making a simple base for the coil pots and make six coils for the project.
2. To create clay coil swirls, start by cutting a length of clay coil and curling it into a swirl shape. Like with other clay coils, it's important to blend the inner layer of the swirl. It's easier to do this by smoothing the back of the swirl before attaching it to the container. Use a tool and your thumb to even out one edge of the swirl. Once smoothed, you can attach the swirl to the coil pot using the slip-and-score technique, which we will go over in more detail in Chapter 8.
3. Then follow the blending technique to attach the back of the swirl to the coil pot, and once the swirl is firmly blended with the pot, move forward to make other swirls.
4. Continue building more coils. Ensure that each coil you make is firmly secured to the pot with the help of the slip and score or blend method. All along the way, you may use your imagination and creativity to add patterns and designs to your pot.

Method #3: Mold

Using a mold to build a coil pot is another method we'll go over.

1. Pick a bowl of your choice as a mold for a coil bowl. *An important tip: Take a simple bowl with a smooth surface to work conveniently.*
2. Wrap your bowl or mold with cling film since it can cover projects evenly. The smoother the plastic covering on the mold, the lesser the chances of developing a creased design on your coils. (Using the cling film simplifies detaching the pot from the bowl after completion.) If you shape the coil pot directly on the bowl, it may be difficult to separate it

while still damp. It's crucial to detach it while still damp to allow for cleaning before the clay becomes firm as it dries. Moreover, cling wrap also prevents the clay from drying.

3. Since you use the bowl as a mold and must press the coil against the bowl, any design (or cling wrap crease) on its exterior or interior will imprint the clay.

4. Make the coils ready, and then start constructing the bowl. You can use the design of your choice in this coiling technique. Try coils, swirls, dots, balls, waves, or blocks. You can arrange them in a regular pattern or make your design more intricate and complex.

5. Cut a coil segment to give it a shape and design of your choice. Then stick it on the bowl with very light slipping and scoring to secure these attachments.

6. Continue building your pattern by adding more coils. Press the coils firmly on top of the stack so that they stick properly. Keep the coils smooth and tidy so that you will finish the project efficiently and on time.

7. After finishing the process, blend the outer surface of the bowl with a wooden tool. Cover the gaps in between coils with extra clay.

8. After blending, the bowl will be smooth. Initially, you can smooth the surface with a metal rib. Next, exert pressure on the clay, enhancing compression and a highly polished surface.

9. The last step is to separate the coil bowl from the mold by peeling the cling film and coil bowl off the mold.

Method #4: Smooth Coil Pottery

In this segment, you will understand the craft well as you will learn to make coil pots on a smooth surface. Start by making a simple coil pot.

1. Flatten a piece of clay having a thickness of approximately 3/4 of an inch. Afterward, carve a round shape from the clay slab to construct the base of the container.

2. You must use the slip-and-score method to build the container's sides or walls. Though it is like creating a basic

coiled vessel, the contrast lies in the fact that while making a basic coiled vessel, the inner surface of the pottery is blended. In contrast, in a polished coiled vessel, the inner and outer surfaces of the coiled pottery are smoothed. The outer surface is smoothed with a wooden tool and the coil ends are joined. A rubber rib is used to tidy the blended area.

3. Continue constructing the height of the vessel by adding more coils. Use a wooden tool, give diagonal strokes, and blend the outer surface of the container. With each coil, keep stroking in alternate directions. As you blend the clay in different directions of every coil, you add strength to the pot.

4. Adding coils gives you the advantage of changing the container. As previously explained, incorporating coils slightly toward the outer perimeter of the coil beneath will expand the size of your container. Alternatively, the pot will narrow if you add coils at the inner edge. As the pot becomes narrow on top, it gets a neck-like shape.

5. Once the shape is given to the container and you are happy with the result, start blending it. Smooth the outer surface with the help of a metal rib. The metal rib helps to get rid of the lumps and bumps on the surface and scrapes off the excess clay. A rubber rib can help to smooth the pot by pressing its surface.

6. You will get to see the final shape of your project. However, you can build the neck of the pot by giving it a twisted asymmetrical shape. The angled neck opening procedure remains unchanged from the earlier coiling method. Incorporate additional clay into the neck by attaching additional coils and seamlessly integrating them. However, the distinction lies in the fact that every extra coil will cover only a part of the neck. As a result, the side with additional coils starts to appear like a neck and produces an asymmetrical look. Keep blending each coil with the previous layer.

7. Once you get the desired shape of your pot, it is ready. It would be best to allow it to sit till it is leather-hard. Once the pot is leather-hard, you can process it with the smoothing process. Here, you may use a scraping tool and sponge to eliminate uneven parts in your piece.

8. The surface will acquire a rough look as you scrape off uneven areas and must be smoothed again. Use a metal rib and a rubber kidney to smooth the rough areas. This shall give a smooth finish to your pot. Use your sponge to give a tidier look to the neck of the pot with the help of ribs and wooden tools.

Method #5: Themed Coil Pot

The best part about coiled pottery is that you can also use the craft to make themed pieces. So, why not learn the skill?

1. We are about to make a rabbit-themed pot using the coil pottery technique. The pot shall begin with crafting the base. The base is given the shape of a rabbit's base. After making the base, you need to construct the pot's sides.
2. As you give the shape of the rabbit's body to the pot, you move ahead and reach the part where you must design its head. Make a coil that is shorter than the rim of the pot. In this manner, a gap forms at a particular spot on the container, where the head can be affixed.
3. Make the rabbit's head after constructing the size and shape of the coil pot body. The head is made with a firm piece of clay. As a result, once the head has been made, it needs a chunk to be scooped out from the base. Remember that solid, moist chunks of clay explode in the kiln. Creating a hollowed head will allow it to dry thoroughly and prevent cracking and explosions while baking.
4. To fix the head, you should eliminate some of the excess clay near the neck region. Afterward, apply the slip and score technique to firmly attach the head (hollowed part) to the pot's body. Use the blending technique to make the attachment smooth. Use a little more clay to smooth the process. This shall ensure that cracks do not develop in the piece while it is dried.
5. Tidy the rim after fixing the head to the body of the pot. A sharp modeling tool followed by a rubber rib will tidy the area. Smoothing the area shall provide a good base for attaching the lid.

6. To make the cover for the container, insert soft fabrics covered with a plastic bag into the hollow space of the rabbit's body. This serves as a support for the cover while you make the lid using the coil pottery technique.

7. Now, wrap a piece of cling film and wrap it at the top of the rabbit's body. Cling film will prevent the soft clay lid from sticking to the pot's body. Next, use the same coil pottery method of slip, score, and blend to make the lid that fits the pot's body. By gradually reducing the size of the clay coils, shape the lid to match the contour of the pot's body.

8. To ensure that the lid stays in place when it covers the pot, coil some clay and attach it to the underside of the lid. Use modeling tools to shape the coils in the underside of the lid.

9. Make some final features to the body of the pot. Incorporate elements like paws, a tail, and a few ears. Use your hand to make and shape the ears and fasten them to the lid through the slip, score, and blend technique. By fixing the ears to the lid instead of the head, they work as handles for the lid. Finally, smooth the whole pot body before drying, followed by firing. While drying, allow the cling wrap to sit between the body and its lid. The lid must be completely dry before removing the cling wrap so that the body and the lid fit easily.

How to Make Coil Pots Using Flat Coils

For centuries, many regions in Asia and Southeast Asia have practiced creating big containers using flat coils. In Korea, skilled potters produce numerous flat-coiled storage jars, which are traditionally used to store kimchi, the country's famous dish composed of pickled veggies seasoned with garlic, red pepper, and ginger. Once you've learned the fundamental technique, crafting sizable jars or any functional or artistic object using the flat coil method becomes feasible.

A significant benefit of this technique is the ability to make substantial changes in direction by allowing the flat coils to become leather-hard. Additionally, you can create a wide range of sculptural shapes. This approach is also time-efficient, employing 2-inch flat coils instead of small circular ones.

It is highly efficient to work in a sequence. Create a set of three to six rows of "loops" on multiple pottery boards simultaneously. Once you complete the last one, you can commence working on the first one again.

1. On a slab roller, roll the clay about ⅛–1/4 inch bigger than the intended thickness of the walls. After smoothing and shaping, the walls will become slimmer. For a sizable jar, slice the clay into even, flat coils with a width of 2 inches.
2. Moisten the pottery board slightly using a sponge before laying the initial flat coil. Secure the first flat coil firmly and then attach another. As you construct the lower part of the jar upside down, position the flat coil on the inner side of the preceding one. The diameter will decrease with each successive row.
3. Furthermore, line the container's interior with plastic to retain moisture. Ensure to make the joints both internally and externally smooth during construction.
4. Allow the initial rows to acquire the leather-hard consistency to ensure they can bear the load of further coils. After the bottom section has hardened, cover it with plastic to prevent it from drying out while you work on it. After the lower section of the vessel is completed, has settled, and stiffened, it's necessary to reinforce the walls.
5. Carve a round shape from a block of clay to form the base of the container. Now, slip and score to attach the base to the piece.
6. Use a paddle to strengthen the seam. Then, cover the item and let it reinforce overnight. This process also helps to balance the moisture level.
7. On the following day, invert the container and make indentations and attach the rim. As the shape has settled and stiffened, affix a tiny circular piece of clay to the edge.
8. Add more flat coils and put the jar right side up to fix the shoulder to the jar.
9. Now, make the rim of the jar by cutting it from the clay slab and attaching it to the jar. Your piece is ready.

How to Fix Pottery That Has Been Dried Unevenly

The extent of shrinkage during the drying process varies depending on the type of clay used, ranging from 2% to 10%, and this does not encompass the shrinkage that arises after employing a kiln to bake your creation. Clay with high shrinkage is more susceptible to cracking. Even drying clayware is a significant process that requires a complete understanding of the diverse drying stages to obtain desired results.

Test your Clay

Evaluating your clay is an exceedingly crucial aspect in ascertaining its drying process. It provides insight into the consistency and composition of your clay and enables you to gauge its drying speed and calculate the degree of contraction upon complete drying. Additionally, you can determine the shrinkage of the piece post-firing.

Sun-Drying

Natural drying is one of the best ways to ensure that your pottery dries, but the process can lead to uneven drying of the piece. Uneven drying is dangerous, as it leads to breakage during firing. The best option is to allow your pot to dry in a shaded area so the entire piece can dry evenly.

Flat Clay Projects or Large Pieces

Plywood coated with newspaper is the most straightforward technique to dry big or flat clay objects evenly. Due to warpage, particleboard is less effective, and drywall might dry the clay too quickly.

How to Tell That Your Pottery Has Dried

The best way to determine that your pottery piece is dried is when its color turns lighter upon drying. Moreover, the piece will weigh lighter because complete drying leads to a loss of 20% moisture in the piece. The easiest way to test the dryness of your pot is to hold it against your skin—if it feels cold, it is not completely dry, and if it feels room temperature, the piece is completely dried.

Coil Pottery Projects

You will find the whole thing more interesting when you learn about the following projects that can be formed with coil pottery. Since it does not require a potter wheel, coil pottery is even more easy and fun to execute at home. So, let's find out.

Plates

Learning to make coil pottery plates is the most fundamental. To create a basic plate, you only need to form a lengthy coil and wrap it around itself. To achieve optimal outcomes, ensure that the coil has a uniform thickness.

You may also interweave multiple coils rotating in diverse directions to obtain a greater variety of ornamental plates. Doing so allows you to produce numerous elaborate designs that are unfeasible to achieve with a pottery machine.

Ensure that all the independent pieces are adequately adhered to; otherwise, these may fall apart when you pick up the plate.

Flower pots

Flower pots are another interesting yet straightforward project that can be made with simple clay coiling. Take a small clay slab and carve it to give a circular shape to form the base of your project. Use a rolling pin to give the circular shape. Make several different coils of the same thickness and length and maintain the same length as the circumference of the base. The trivial part is keeping the coils' height (stacks) without collapsing.

Mugs and Cups

Since you have learned to make stacks, you can make mugs and cups now. This project is much smaller than creating flower pots. It would help if you made thinner coils, and at the same time, you must ensure that these coils do not tear because they are fragile.

Stacking coils will give you a cup; if you add a handle, you get a mug. To ensure that the project does not allow liquid to leak, smooth down the coils inside the cup or mug.

Decorative vases

These ornamental vases utilize identical design tricks like dishes. You can transform an uninteresting container into a stunning vase by merely incorporating a couple of twists while layering the coils. Since this project is more complex than the ones mentioned above, it is best to start with the more straightforward designs and graduate with this one.

If your vase repeatedly falls apart, you could utilize an old vase that is no longer in use and employ it as a support structure to enfold the coils around.

Fruit bowl

Why not try to make a fruit bowl with raised edges? The simplest way to attain this impact is by utilizing a large container already in your possession. Wrap the container with some plastic material and insert the clay coils and twists inside the container.

Your fruit bowl will have the same shape as the mold used by you. After finishing the design and drying process, carefully remove the mold before firing.

Coiled pitcher

Since you already know how to make cups and mugs, this project is simply an extension of the same project. The significant difference in this project is to make the lip of the pitcher. You may add decorations to the pitcher as you desire.

Coasters

Use the same technique of creating a spiral plate. By maintaining sufficient distance between coils or twists, you can generate pockets of air that aid in cooling any object placed on your coasters.

Woven coil pots

Watch out for the most interesting part of coil pottery. In this design, you get the opportunity to weave your coils to form a weaved coil pot.

Basic round coils are a fundamental way to begin coil pottery but not the only limitation. Flat and triangle coils are equally interesting to learn and master the skill.

Having gained familiarity with the art of coil pottery, it's time to venture into the captivating realm of slab pottery. Let's dive right in and get started.

6

SLAB POTTERY

So it is with Lee Davids, a potter specializing in slab pottery, a technique in which slabs of clay are hand-shaped into completed platters, plates, and bowls. The unique part about his work is that all his pieces are slab-built because he prefers the unstructured, freeform, dynamic, and natural forms of construction using slabs. So, what is slab pottery?

Slab Pottery

Slab construction ceramics is a method of creating hand-built pieces by joining walls together using the slip-and-score technique. Slab ceramics are generally more geometric in shape than other conventional pottery projects. This method requires constructing "walls" for a container, followed by slipping and scoring the clay where the walls will meet. Ultimately, the walls are joined together to form the final piece.

Currently, flat containers and the method of creating them with flat sheets are gaining renewed interest. Contemporary pottery makers and artists working with ceramics have adopted the slab technique, producing pieces with pliable and firm leather-hard sheets.

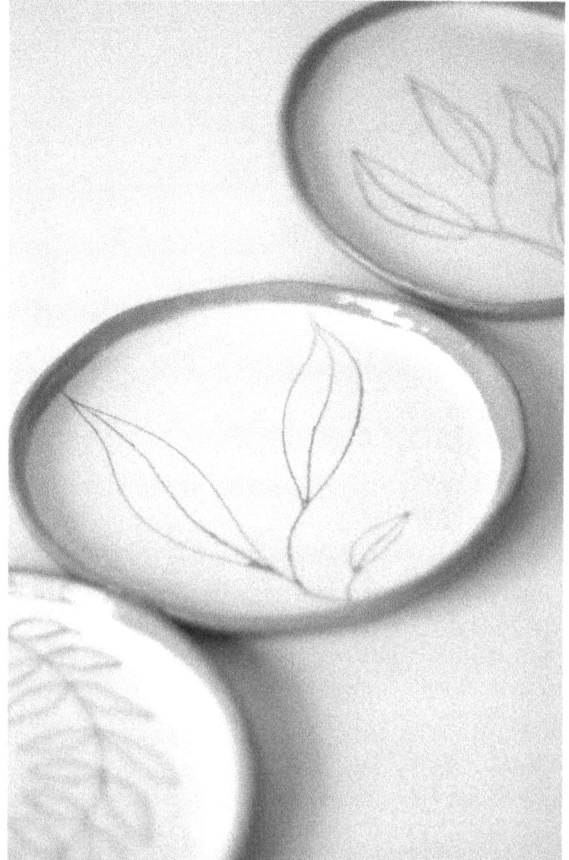

Slab Pottery Techniques

Creating pottery by constructing it manually using clay slabs is a thrilling technique to form designs that cannot be crafted through a potter's wheel or may pose a challenge when shaping by hand using clay coils. Your hand and the type of clay you use for the artistry are the two main parameters that can play a decisive role in this craft.

Making slabs

Though slab rollers, extruders, and hand tossing are good techniques for rolling a slab of clay, hand rolling with a rolling pin is still the most basic one to make a slab with clay.

When working with a sizable amount of clay, slab rollers can be a valuable tool to assist you—these large pieces of equipment aid in creating uniformly thick slabs. However, you can opt for the hand-tossing method if you prefer a more rustic and handmade aesthetic. This technique adds an organic touch by gently tossing the slab onto a sturdy surface, giving your work with a unique and natural feel.

- Soft-slab construction

Ceramic artists have embraced a technique where they use freshly rolled wet slabs. These flexible slabs can be shaped into elegant structures reminiscent of leather. They can be used with molds to create consistent shapes, allowing artists to focus on adding surface designs, embellishments, or firing techniques. Furthermore, the soft slabs can be shaped and then integrated into larger pieces once they have reached the leather-hard stage.

- Stiff slab construction

This method is more suitable and applicable for geometrical and architectural shapes. The slab is rolled out and made leather-hard to cut and combine with another stiffened piece to get the desired form.

Other leather-hard clay components that are stiff, slump-molded slabs, thrown components, or pinched components can be integrated with stiff slab forms. As part of making a cover for the pot, a soft slab may be slumped into the opening of the stiff slab pot. Another alternative is to create a series of rings and place them on the bottom of the pot to function as feet. There are endless possibilities, with creativity being the limit.

How to Make a Basic Slab Pot

1. Create a slab

Form a thick slurry. (Allow some clay pieces to dry completely for a few days before placing them in a jar with sufficient water to cover them completely. They will immediately combine to form a slurry.) By utilizing slurry instead of water, you boost the joint's strength throughout the construction process as well as over the life of the pot.

Slabs can be pressed out to create small pots using a simple method. Begin by taking a clay lump approximately two inches in diameter. Use your palms to compress the ball as much as possible, and then press it down on a surface to compress it further until it reaches a consistent thickness of ¼ to ½ inch. Finally, carefully lift the slab from the work surface.

2. Make the base of your slab pot

Trim the slab you just made with your potter's needle. Although you can create a base of any size or shape, I recommend making your first slab pot's foundation a two-inch-by-two-inch square. (It does not have to be a perfect square or dimensions.)

Gently refine the trimmed edges of your square by delicately tapping each edge on your work area. Employing your potter's pin, mark (or scrape) the top surface of the slab along every edge. Your marking should be at most 1/4 inch in width and 1/16 inch in depth.

3. Construct the initial and secondary surfaces of your clay vessel

Form a slab in the same manner as in step one. Using the potter's needle, cut one edge into a straight line. Mark and trim away the clay so the new slab is the same width as the old one, laying it against one side of your foundation. Trim the upper edge to the desired height of the completed pot. Make a second slab and cut it to the same measurements as the first.

4. Attach the slab pot's first two sides

Make shallow cuts on the lower edge of the side slab. On the side that will become the inside of the final vessel, make similar cuts along the two lateral edges. With your sumi brush, delicately apply a thin layer of clay and water mixture along the cuts on one of the edges of the base slab. Carefully place the side slab in an upright position into the moistened cut.

Ideally, the side slab should be in a position to stay upright, but, if it falls, support it using any hand or handy object. Make a little coil, about 1/16 inch in diameter. Place it along and into the internal corner created by the base and side slabs. Lightly press and attach the coil to the base and side slabs with the curved tip of your wooden tool. Leave any leftover coil length connected but loose.

Repeat this procedure with the remaining side slab, scoring the internal surface.

5. Make the last two sides of the slab pot

Repeat steps one and three to make a slab. Use a potter's needle to make and trim a straight line at one edge. Mark and trim away the clay so the new slab fits neatly between the inner surfaces of the two sides already in place so it faces one edge of your base. Cut the top edge to the desired height of the completed pot. Trim the same way as a second slab.

6. Attach the remaining sides of the slab

Mark the lower and side edges of one of the side blocks. With your sumi brush, softly apply a layer of slurry along the marking on each border. Carefully place the lateral block vertically into the gap formed by the initial two slabs.

Arrange any remaining coil from connecting the initial two slabs so that it ascends along the side seam. If it falls short, roll and position another piece of coil to cover the entire joint length between the side slabs. Gently press and fuse the spiral to both side slabs with the help of the round tip of your wooden tool while supporting the pot from the outside with one hand. Repeat the process for the joints on the bottom and the opposite side. Repeat this process with the final side slab, ensuring you mark the internal surface.

7. Finish the basic slab pot

For extra protection from fractures and fragmentation, delicately fuse the external layer of every connection by utilizing the curved tip of a wooden instrument. With great care, hold your pot inclined to your work surface and softly strike the lower borders to even out the surface and produce a slightly slanting edge where you will place the pot on a table. (This slight incline provides the pot with a visual elevation, which is aesthetically pleasing.)

While using the potter's needle, even out the pot's upper edge. To prevent the sides of your pot against the pressure of the needle, support them with your fingers. Smooth the upper part with slip and run them evenly all over. Join and smooth each top joint with your fingers, supporting the clay with one hand while applying pressure with the other

Once the pot is dried, it is ready for bisque fire. After bisque firing, your piece is good to be glazed, and then you can place it in the kiln for the glaze firing.

Slab Pottery Projects

Here are some excellent slab pottery projects to try.

Decorative Leaf Bowl

Using slab pottery, create a trinket to hold your jewelry pieces, clips, keys, or buttons. So, here is the easy method to make a decorative leaf bowl.

- Look out for a fresh leaf of your choice as the template for the design.
- Take wax paper and roll out a block of clay on it of about 7 mm thickness so that it does not break.
- Now, lay the leaf on the clay so that it leaves its imprint on it. Remove it after a while.
- Take a sharp knife to cut the border of the leaf imprint and remove the excess clay.
- Put your slab in a bowl to dry. Alternatively, you may maintain it flat with realistic curled edges by forming a ring

with aluminum foil and curling the overlapping edges up or down.

- For complete drying of the clay, ensure that you dry it for two days, flipping the sides daily.
- If you want to give it a professional finesse, opt for the sanding technique with sandpaper. Then apply a layer of satin sealer, and your bowl is complete.

Soap Dish

This dish is identical to the previous one but significantly more challenging. Choose a smaller leaf with a sturdy stem this time. Consider rolling out the clay thicker to construct a more lasting dish.

- After you've cut out your leaf pattern, stack it on a higher level on a flat surface, such as a book covered with wax paper.
- Hollow out the stem using a modeling tool, as this will serve as the drainage part of the soap dish.
- Taper the wrinkled stem over the book's exterior, ensure it touches the wax paper, and set it aside to dry.
- To create a durable product, bisque-fire the dish.

Cell Phone Holder Scrolls (Textured)

These are useful pieces, as they can hold your cell phone in place while you put them on charge. It is essential to ensure that the piece is the right size for your phone and effectively prevents it from falling.

- Roll out clay about 5 mm thick on wax paper.
- Take a rectangle of 30 cm x 5 cm and cut the clay to take the desired measurement.
- Allow the clay to lay flat on a textured material.
- Roll a short piece of newspaper inside each end of your scroll to keep its shape.
- Tuck extra newspaper on both sides of your rolled-up scrolls to prevent them from unrolling while drying.
- Gently blow your cell phone to rest within the scroll to gauge its fitting.

- You can become more creative with your piece and carve your name (or the one to whom you want to gift it) on the product before it is dry.

Slab Flowerpot

This project will also require the scoring technique and is more technical than the earlier ones.

- Take a slab of clay and roll it out 1 cm thick.
- Make a rectangle 30 cm x 5 cm in dimension and a circle 5 cm in diameter.
- Take a sponge and smooth the clay.
- Join both pieces with the scoring method.
- Make a thin clay cylinder equal in length to the pot's base and score it.
- Create a slip by blending a ball-shaped lump of clay with a small amount of water. The slip shall function as the adhesive to unite everything.
- Coat the edges with a clay coating in the spots where they will connect. Position the cylinder on the circumference of the foundation where it has been marked.
- Wrap the slab of clay around the circle.
- Press the slab's overlapping sides to close them and secure all regions with slip to ensure it is securely in place.
- Crumple newspaper into the pot to preserve its shape while it dries.

Slab Plate

Making slab plates with patterns and textures is an advanced technique that is more difficult than a basic slab plate.

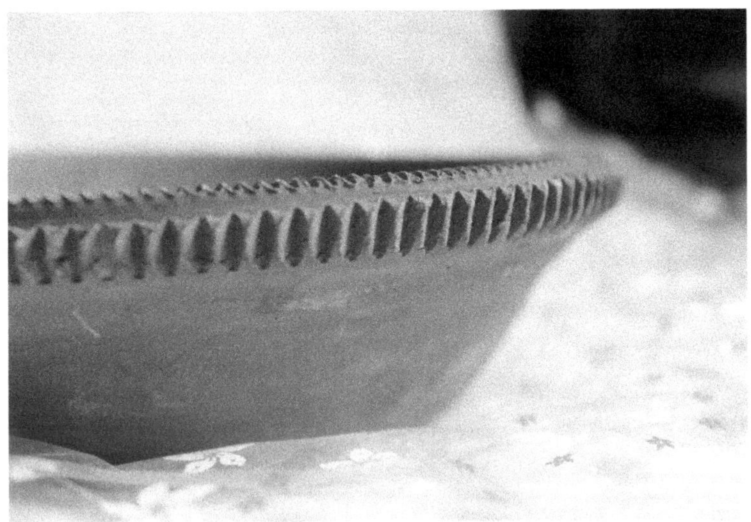

- Flatten your clay to a thickness of 0.5 to 1 centimeter.
- Use a template for the project. Take a paper plate, and using its circumference, cut the clay accordingly.
- Position the circular slab within the plate and place it in between another plate, then exert intense pressure downwards.
- Let the plate dry within the paper plate and then unmold it to get your slab plate. Decorate it as you desire.

Cups of Slab Pottery

Making cups and mugs is a popular craft in pottery. And slab pottery can also produce beautiful mugs and cups.

- Flatten a slab of clay using a rolling pin.
- Form the mug's base by cutting the slab into a circle.
- Take another slab of clay to form a rectangular piece, and perfect it using a ruler and a knife.
- One of the sides should be etched, then wrapped around the circular base with a slip.
- Trim off the extra clay.
- Close the cup by etching and applying another slip.
- Smooth the edges using your fingers.

- Add a handle to the cup and finish your project.

Slab Pottery Trays

Rectangular trays and plates are trendy slab pottery projects.

- Take a big rectangular piece of clay and roll it.
- Cut the slab according to the shape of your choice.
- Bend or curve the side of the rectangular shape to give it the form of a tray.
- If you desire, add some base to the tray.

Slab Pottery Tips

Here are some practical slab pottery tips to help you achieve good results. Try different techniques for building slab pottery and find the one that works the best for you.

Here are the five best tips potters should incorporate while doing slab pottery.

1. **Avoid unwanted texture on your piece by working on an old bedsheet**. Bedsheets with high thread count have little texture, acting as the best working surface for slab pottery. So, the result is an excellent and smooth slab for working.
2. **You should dip the scraps in water and place them in clay bags to reduce the reclaim**. The extra pieces are not wasted and can be wedged again for another project.
3. **Take a large piece of the slab to make a tube-like or cylinder-like shape without warping it**. Gently pick it up from one corner without pulling it or rushing the process. You can hold it in your hands with ease. The piece will stick to your fingers, and you can gently put it on the working surface and give it the desired shape.
4. **Adding too much water is not the correct technique**. A soft slab is good enough to be molded without slipping and scoring. Stiff clay requires slip and

score, but the same is sometimes true for a smooth slab of clay.

5. Another valuable technique is **compressing joints to make seams vanish**. To achieve this, employ overlapping methods to join the beveled parts, ensuring the seam becomes invisible. Apply pressure (you may use your fingers), pushing the lower part away from you and the upper part toward you, resulting in a flawless finish.

Now that you've honed your skills in slab pottery, it's time to delve into the next technique: press mold pottery. The upcoming chapter will open the doors to understanding press mold pottery, where you'll discover a variety of techniques and approaches to this craft.

REVIEW REQUEST

Hey there, fellow pottery enthusiasts! Have you enjoyed this book so far? If so, I'd like to ask you to take a few minutes to share your thoughts and experiences by leaving a review.

Now, you might be wondering, "Why should I bother leaving a review for this book?" Well, my friends, the answer is simple: leaving a review can help others discover the joy of hand-building pottery and experience greater fulfillment in their creative endeavors.

So, let me ask you this: have you ever received a recommendation from a friend that led you to discover something new and exciting? Maybe it was a restaurant, a movie, or a hobby. Whatever it was, you probably felt grateful for the recommendation and wanted to share your positive experience with others.

Leaving a review for "Hand Building Pottery" is a way to pay it forward and help others discover the same joy you have found in hand-building pottery. Your honest feedback can guide others in their decision to purchase the book and start their creative journey.

Furthermore, leaving a review helps to meet a need in the community. When someone is considering purchasing a product, they often turn to reviews to help make their decision. By sharing your experience with "Hand Building Pottery," you can help others make an informed decision and feel confident in their purchase.

If you've enjoyed this book so far, please take a moment to leave an honest review on your preferred platform. This could be Amazon, Goodreads, or any other platform where the book is available.

To leave a review on Amazon, scan this QR code:

From there, you can rate the book and share your thoughts. Sharing your personal experience will genuinely help and encourage others by providing them with an additional perspective on what they can expect to gain from reading this book.

Additionally, your review provides valuable feedback that helps me improve my work and create excellent content. And who knows, you may even introduce someone else to a new hobby that brings them fulfillment and joy!

I appreciate your support, and happy creating!

7

POTTERY USING PRESS MOLDS

Pottery press molds are quite popular and commonly made of plastic or wood. Both plastic and wood materials allow the clay to dry and release from the molds without hassle. Hand-building pottery is cost-intensive, but the process is laborious, and if the potter is an amateur, then the chances of producing identical pieces are challenging. Press molds can come to their rescue in such cases.

What Is a Press Mold?

The press molding technique involves pressing clay into a mold to take on its shape and then removing it to create a replica of the mold. This method is beneficial for producing numerous identical pieces and is common for making plates, bowls, cups, and tiles. Press molds are also known as spring molds.

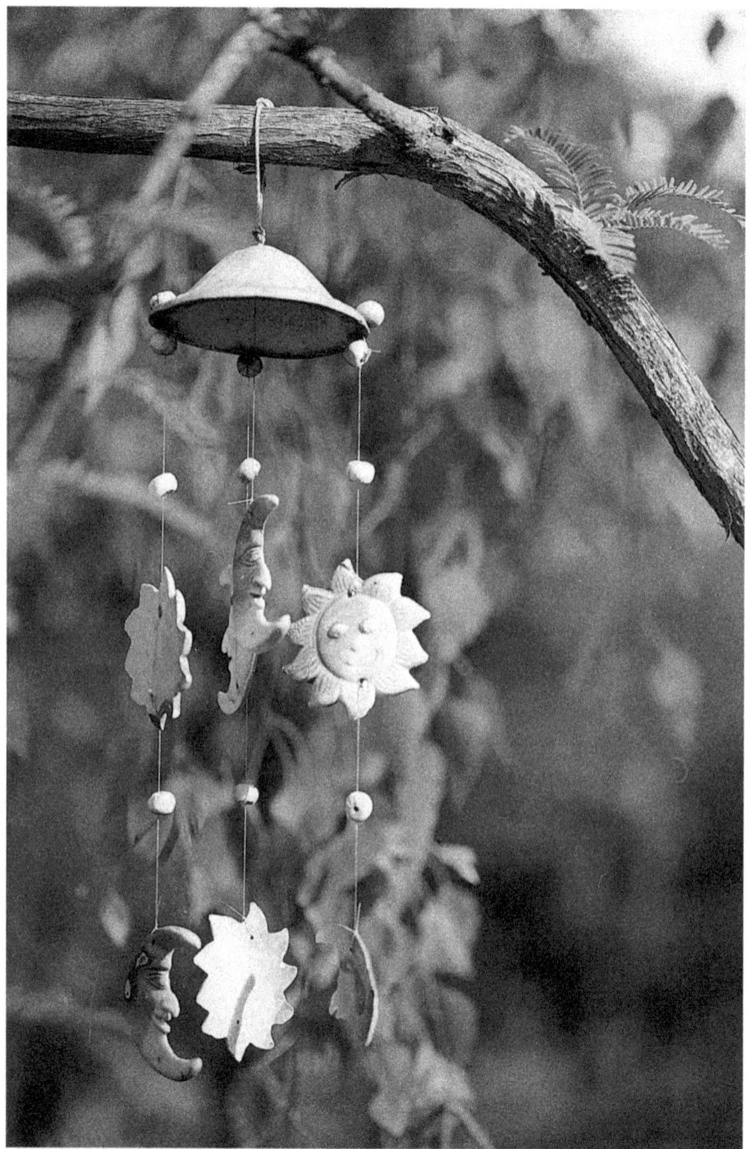

Types of Press Molds

Plaster cast and **bisque** are the two different types of press molds. Plaster cast press molds are formed by combining plaster of Paris with talc, which reduces the chance of cracking. The liquid is dropped into a rubber mold for setting. Plaster cast press molds are burned to eliminate the water content at a far lower temperature than ceramics.

The second category of press mold, the bisque mold, is a preferred option since you can conveniently make it at home. Just ensure that you roll out the clay uniformly to your desired thickness and then utilize any object of your choice to shape the mold, ranging from plates and mugs to cake tins. Nevertheless, covering the mold with a lining (for example, talc powder, cornstarch, tap water, or pantyhose) is essential to prevent the clay from adhering and allow it to dry to a leather-hard consistency.

You may also use wet clay to **slip cast molds** or make your mold over Styrofoam, which works well if you're carving your own pattern onto it. Finally, you may make your own forms by pressing shells, fossils, or pebbles into the clay.

A **hump mold** is arched (convex), implying that the cast protrudes outward in a hump form. A piece of pottery can then be hung over the hump and shaped around it. As the pottery hardens, it maintains the mold's shape. A **slump mold** has a concave configuration. It curves inward, and the clay slab is pressed into the depressed shape. Like the hump mold, the clay takes on the mold's form as it strengthens.

Uses of Press Molds

Press mold is a simple technique to learn and execute— ensure your clay is rolled out uniformly to the desired thickness and lay it on top of the mold. Once the clay has been formed into the mold, let it mature to become leather-hard before extracting it from the mold, but be cautious while removing the clay because the clay is extremely fragile at this time. Trim any extra clay from the mold's edges and ensure that all your edges are neat and organized before firing.

Press molds are effective in duplicating vast amounts of a particular ceramic variety. They are also valuable for creating embossed designs that are frequently observed in the renowned Wedgwood pottery established by Josiah Wedgwood. Using press molds, you can produce delicate ceramic accessories such as beads and pendants.

Press Mold Techniques

The Press mold pottery is quite like creating bisque-fired mold. You can make it yourself. The first step is to roll the slab of clay on your working surface and then place it on the desired mold. Remember that the thickness should be ideal because thin slabs of clay are susceptible to breakage while accommodating them in the molds. Line the mold because the clay may stick to the mold, making it challenging to remove. Then the extra clay will need trimming before removing your piece from the mold. Your pottery is ready for bisque-firing and glazing.

Slumping and Draping Molds

You already know that slump molds and hump molds are two typical methods for shaping slabs into shapes. Clay is put into the mold in slump molds. The clay slab is placed over the mold in hump molds.

- Materials for mold

Plaster, wood, foam board, bisque clay, upholstery foam, and similar materials are used to create molds. You can utilize almost any material; however, there will be constraints because clay contracts as it dries.

Hump molds must be flexible enough to accommodate clay contraction. Slump molds have fewer limitations since the clay shrinks away from the mold rather than toward its surface.

Pages of a newspaper should be positioned between the clay slab and the mold in both types of molds if a non-porous material is chosen. Otherwise, the clay may not come out clean of the mold.

- Slump molding

You can create plates, bowls, trays, or platters by bending a flat piece of clay into a pre-existing dish or plate. This technique is most effective for low-profile shapes. For deeper bowls, the clay slab will require trimming to eliminate excess clay and create a seamless fit in the mold. An alternative approach is connecting multiple slabs in the mold to achieve the desired form. In both instances, you must securely fuse the slabs.

A different variety of slump molds is the open-center mold. These enable the form to be shaped by the inherent curve of the slab. Molds, frequently constructed from plywood or foam, are relatively high and have a sizable opening in the center. A huge slab is placed on top, after which the mold is lifted and softly lowered to prompt the clay to settle in the middle.

- Drape the clay over the mold

As a result of the clay's shrinkage, it is advisable to construct hump molds from absorbent and adaptable substances. In addition to the materials mentioned above, a temporary mold can be fashioned by a crumpled newspaper or fabric and enclosing them in a plastic wrap or pouch.

If the hump pattern can be compressed along with the clay, it facilitates the incorporation of feet or a foot ring when the clay is still pliable. However, if the mold cannot compress, you must remove the clay before it reaches the leather-hard phase. In such a scenario, adding feet is not feasible, as the principal portion of the vessel would cave in if any additions were attached to its base.

Pottery becomes more engaging and thrilling if you embellish your project with different materials (beads, stones, adding patterns and textures, etc.). The following chapter will take you through the techniques employed to embellish your craft.

$$8$$

EMBELLISHMENT AND JOINING CLAY

Pottery is a versatile art; adding embellishments to the ceramics can produce delightful results. Different techniques are utilized to embellish pieces, air-drying clay being one of them.

Rules for Joining Clay

Clay should be wet

The greater the amount of water amid the clay particles, the greater their capacity to move and mix. When clay pieces are soft and pliable, they are simple to integrate and physically bond to form a single piece.

Adjoining like with like

When connecting clay components, they must be uniformly moist (possess identical moisture levels). As the clay dries, it contracts—the liquid state between the clay particles vaporizes, and the clay particles come closer to each other.

When a moist clay piece is attached to a comparatively dry clay piece, the moist clay piece still has additional shrinkage to undergo than the drier piece. Therefore, as it experiences more shrinkage, it generates tension and strives to break away from the arid piece.

Novice artists may unknowingly join a moist chunk of clay to an almost bone-dry piece, and the damp clay will contract more than the drier clay, and all their hard work will be futile.

The simplest method is to moisten the drier component or dry off the wetter component before combining them. These steps are necessary until the sections are uniformly moist and then join them. If you heed this rule, you will save the frustration of joining components in pottery.

Soft, moist clay fragments, such as clay coils used in pottery, can be united by physically amalgamating the pieces, crushing and fusing them into each other at the juncture. Pieces of wet clay that are merely laid on each other or softly pressed together will cling together at first, but as the clay dries, they will come apart. Pieces must be firmly conjoined together or scored and slipped to stay linked when burned in a kiln.

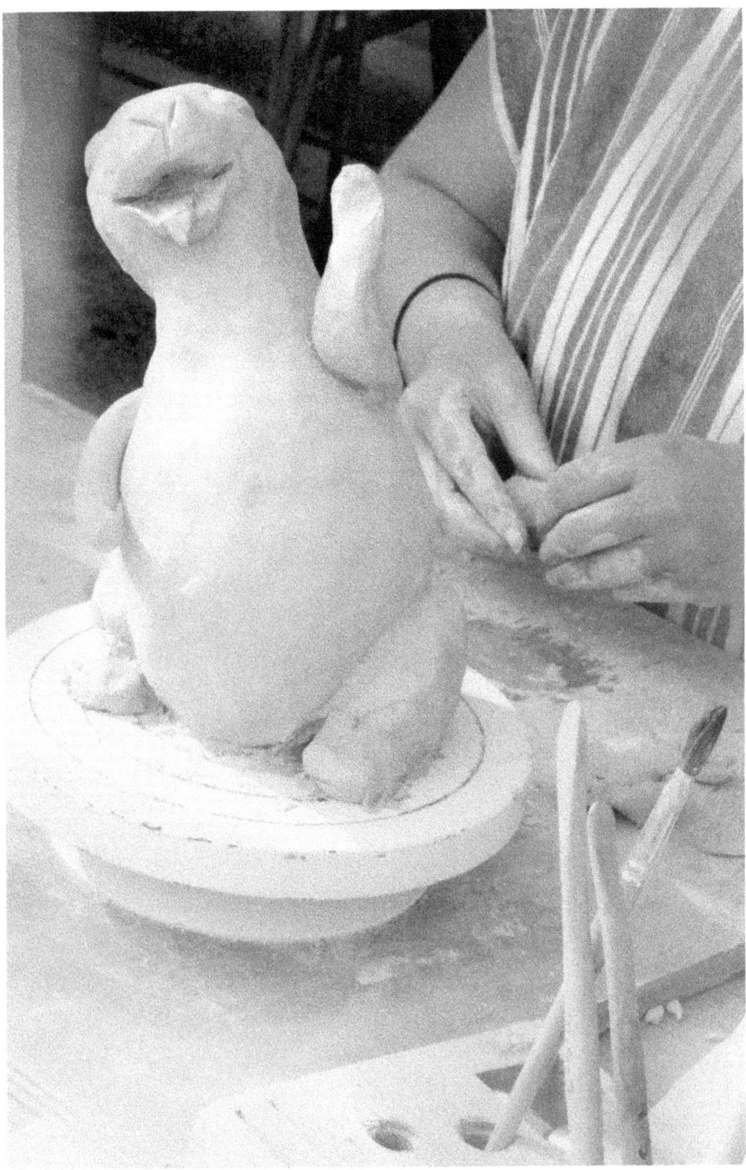

Scoring and Slipping

Traditionally, when dealing with clay pieces that are dry and firm or need to be joined together without changing their shapes, one must use the method of scoring and slipping. Slip helps to bind the pieces together. Unless you have tried and tested what suits you best, slipping and scoring is relatively foolproof when executed accurately. So, let's understand the steps.

- Mark the spot where you want to join the pieces.
- Utilizing a serrated scraper, for example, a fork, needle tool, blade, or any other sharp instrument, creates furrows in the clay. Create a crosshatch pattern with the furrows and ensure they are deeper than superficial marks.
- Use your finger, knife, or brush to spread the slip on the scored marks. Be cautious while filling the grooves so air pockets are not created. Certain ceramic artists invert this technique by applying slip first and then scoring it, thus slicing the slip into the clay.
- If the clay is relatively dry at the leather-hard stage, it is advisable to rescore and reapply the slip to ensure thorough integration and enhance the sticking of the parts.
- Once you have slipped and scored both pieces, it's advisable to allow them to rest for a brief period until the moist gloss of the slot becomes less shiny. This will enhance their adhesive properties and decrease their slipperiness when you join them.
- Firmly attach the pieces. Tap down on one component over the connection or wiggle it slightly while you push it to facilitate its placement and eliminate any air pockets.
- Always double-check that you've set up everything as you intend—you only have a few seconds to make changes. If you're putting numerous parts together, such as in a slab vessel, be sure the piece you just joined hasn't thrown off the previously attached ones.
- Clean away remaining slip, wipe fingerprints, and rejoin parts as needed. When done, the linked portions will be wetter than the rest of the piece; to balance the moisture, cover the item in plastic and set it aside for a few minutes before proceeding.
- When the joints in slab vessels are solid, it might be a pleasant touch to roll a tiny coil of clay and push it into the inner corners of the connections to make them more appealing and to help them remain together.

Alternative Solutions to Slip

Vinegar

Because clay is a bit alkaline, vinegar's acidic nature acts as a clay binder. Use it on both sides and immediately push the pieces together without slipping or scoring.

Magic mud or paper clay slip

You can prepare this mixture by using materials like toilet paper ($\frac{1}{2}$ or $\frac{1}{3}$ roll) and bone-dry clay ($\frac{2}{3}$ to $\frac{3}{4}$). Place the clay and paper into a container and pour magic water until the level reaches about an inch higher than the clay and paper. Allow the mixture to rest overnight, and the following morning use a blender to blend the stuff after draining the excess water. Your slip-like material is ready to use on leather-hard pieces. Alternatively, dry it to make a putty that you can use to patch the cracks in the details.

In case of graver problems in connecting or mending shattered bone-dry clay fragments or even bisque-fired pieces, or to ensure that the connections between leather-hard slabs remain intact, you can use a mixture of paper, clay, and magic water, vinegar, and other combinations. The paper fibers in the mix hold things together against drying pressure, making rewetting and drying faster and simpler. The solution will need continuous mixing as and when required because if it is mixed and left unused for a prolonged period, it disintegrates and sinks.

Attaching Clay Parts

In this next section, we will go through the techniques for attaching dry and wet clay parts.

Wet Parts

Scoring and slipping are essential pottery techniques. Using a fork or a needle tool, water, or slip, the potters score both the piece's sides that require bonding.

Dry Parts

Attaching two pieces that have surpassed the leather-hard stage is challenging. Occasionally, you may employ a branded adhesive like Magic Mender or **APTII** adhesive to affix sections of unfired clay or bisque. These can secure, repair and produce decorative finishes on surfaces. After application, these substances bond easily and quickly.

Wrapping wet newspaper over the finished piece before wrapping it in plastic is a final technique for facilitating the adequate adhesion of wet and dry clay. This method helps distribute moisture throughout the item, resulting in less cracking.

Crafting successful pottery items requires excellent care and attention to detail. It's crucial to strictly follow each step in the process, including the proper drying techniques and methods. Rushing through the drying cycles is not recommended, as it can ruin your project. In the next chapter, we'll dive into the various drying phases and the correct procedures to ensure your pottery is dried adequately and prepared for the first firing.

9

DRYING CLAY STAGES

D rying the clay is a significant stage that helps to achieve excellent results. Beginners need to know the correct technique for drying their clay. In this lesson, we will discuss the drying stages of pottery.

Factors Influencing the Drying Process of Pottery

After shaping and designing your pottery, it is essential to ensure it is thoroughly dry before the firing process. This crucial step ensures the final outcome of your pottery piece is maintained, avoiding fragile, cracked, or even broken pottery once it enters the kiln. The fundamental principle is to dry the pottery gradually and consistently to ensure complete drying. Here are the factors that impact the drying process of pottery.

Climate

The rule of thumb is to allow enough time for your piece to dry. If you live in a place characterized by humidity, giving your piece a week extra than the usual drying time is best. Such vigilance is necessary to overcome the ill effects of dampness in your pot. The longer time you allot for drying your piece, the better it is.

People staying in places with a dry climate can enjoy the benefit of the climate for their pottery pieces because it ensures faster drying of clay pieces. Even big-size pieces can completely dry within one week. However, a dry climate can also have a negative impact. Sometimes, the piece can become overly dry, and this can also lead to the development of cracks in the clay pot.

Size of the piece

Thick pieces require more time to dry. So, it will need extra time to dry completely. Moreover, the climate of the place plays a significant role too. If the piece is thick and you live in an area with a humid climate, leave your pot for an extra week to dry completely.

Components of the clay

The clay's ingredients also determine the clay piece's drying time. Since different clays have different additives, their drying time varies. Higher water content is present in plastic clays with finer ingredients, for example, porcelain. This means that such type of clay needs extra time for drying and leads to shrinkage while firing. Clay that shrinks is more likely to develop cracks.

The tip in such cases is to add grog because it helps to reduce the shrinkage in clay, thus reducing cracking and promoting the drying process. Grog is pre-fried and has a fine composition. Since the grog is fired, it will not absorb water and initiate the drying process.

Grog has a minor drawback—it makes the clay less malleable. Hence, it is not appropriate for complex undertakings.

Drying Your Clay Piece

Understanding the process of drying your clay piece is integral to learning pottery. Clay undergoes numerous physical and chemical transformations, from moist clay to being glazed, fired, and finally, completed. You can prevent your pieces from cracking and warping by understanding the correct technique of clay drying.

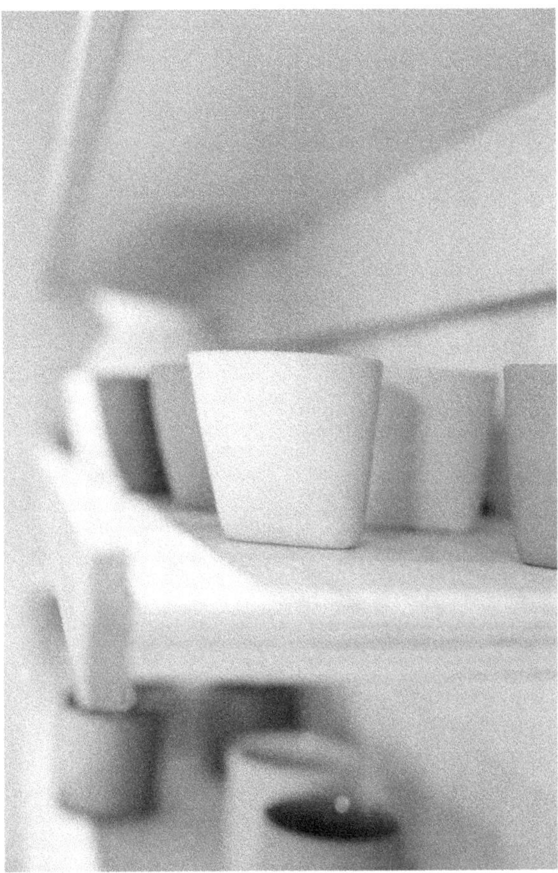

Use shelves for drying

Place your finished piece of pottery on a shelf for uniform drying. Drying clay on a shelf allows circulation of air all around the piece, leading to even drying.

Consider plastic as your unexpected hero

Potters realize the importance of plastic in hand-building pottery. Placing a basic plastic covering over items that require a substantial amount of time to dry guarantees a gradual drying process. It shields them from irregular drying caused by being exposed to drafts. However, the dampness from clay drying tends to accumulate in the upper section of plastic coverings, leading to excessive moisture in fragile rims and intricate features.

Adding a cloth or paper towel layer between your piece and the plastic cover can help trap the humidity. Substituting these moist coatings with dry ones at fixed intervals facilitates step-by-step drying and averts exposure to gusts of air that lead to irregular drying.

You may skip the plastic altogether for pieces that can dry faster. Construct a "tent" of cloth or newspaper to keep out unwanted winds while allowing moisture to escape gradually.

Pieces that have attachments like long handles or similar construction should be dried with care because the drying temperature of clay at the different joining points is dissimilar, causing breakage of the attachment or crack development in the piece. Hence, to ensure an equal drying rate of the piece, you may wrap the delicate portion with plastic.

Wrap the edges

Edges are another challenging area in ceramic pieces that are vulnerable to uneven drying, leading to cracks. To safeguard delicate edges, shred plastic strips and position them on the edges of moist pots to slow down the process of drying.

Ceramics with uniform height rims can be flipped over to sit on the rim, transforming the entire object into a seamless, enclosed shape. However, this drying process may pose a risk for incredibly fragile pieces or uneven edges.

Use wired surface for drying clay tiles and slabs

Ceramic tiles and slabs are particularly susceptible to deformation and fracturing, as they typically possess only a single elongated side exposed to the atmosphere, resulting in irregular block drying. One of the best techniques to ensure uneven drying of such pieces is to place them on a wire rack or surface for drying.

You may flatten the piece on a fabric, lift the material from the edges like a sling, and place it on the rack.

Handling the piece this way reduces the possibility of it getting deformed during transportation.

Here are the points to remember for the perfect drying of your pieces.

- Place the plastic sheet on your piece while drying.
- Prevent uneven drying, as this can cause cracks and breakage.
- Flipping the pots upside-down can lead to even drying of the piece.
- To attain an equal drying rate, wrap the delicate parts (like rims and handles) with a plastic covering.
- Avoid drying ceramics forcibly. Using heating devices or blowers, such as hair dryers, can result in significant fissures, mainly when the clay is already leather-hard or drier.

Alternatives to Air-Drying

Substitutes are available to hasten the drying of your clay; however, they carry hazards, as rapid drying may lead to cracks. Despite expediting the process, it is crucial to thoroughly dry the item by proceeding gradually and consistently. The following methods can be employed to achieve a moderately accelerated drying phase.

- **Candling:** To hasten the procedure, take advantage of your electric kiln. The most suitable method is to adjust the temperature to 82 °C and keep it for 8 to 12 hours. Employing the candling technique can eliminate of any excessive dampness from your work uniformly.
- **Heat Gun:** The heat gun can be a helpful technique for drying, but it may result in irregular drying if not applied correctly. Adjust the gun to a relatively mild temperature and execute the procedure for less than 15 minutes to guarantee a more favorable result.
- **Blow Dryers:** Blow dryers can be a helpful tool for assisting the drying process only if used without the heat setting. A blow dryer with a "no heat" setting will ensure even drying results.

- **Fan**: Fans are handy for drying pottery, but they should be positioned so that the air circulates on all sides to even dry the piece.

Clay objects that have been formed but have not yet undergone the process of bisque firing are referred to as greenware. This firing process is essential for the transformation of clay into ceramic. The unfired clay is termed "greenware," which is incredibly delicate.

Greenware has various drying stages: moist, humid, pliable leather-hard, firm leather-hard, rigid leather-hard, arid, and completely parched. During this time, the item can still be altered by adding more clay or dampening it to make it malleable and then remodeling it. Before being subjected to the kiln's heat, unfired pottery be used in its current state.

Greenware Pottery Stages

During the greenware phase, you have molded your ceramic item, assuming it is in its ultimate shape before firing. You subjected the clay substance to all molding and air-elimination methods and subsequently fashioned it into the desired configuration. Greenware is exceedingly delicate, and any collision can impair it, resulting in breakage or distortion.

Greenware is pliable enough to allow adding more water and reshaping. It also accommodates the incorporation of additional components, like a clay handle. However, the drying process remains a significant component of a successful piece.

Drying Greenware

Firing greenware in the kiln is not done to avoid breakage unless it is bone dry. The piece must be completely and evenly dry before entering the kiln. There are better approaches than force-drying greenware. Drying the piece on shelves or racks is preferred. Lids must dry independently from their pots or jars using a paper towel, or they will attach together. The drying process is stage-centric; only when the piece does not feel cold to touch against the skin is it completely dried.

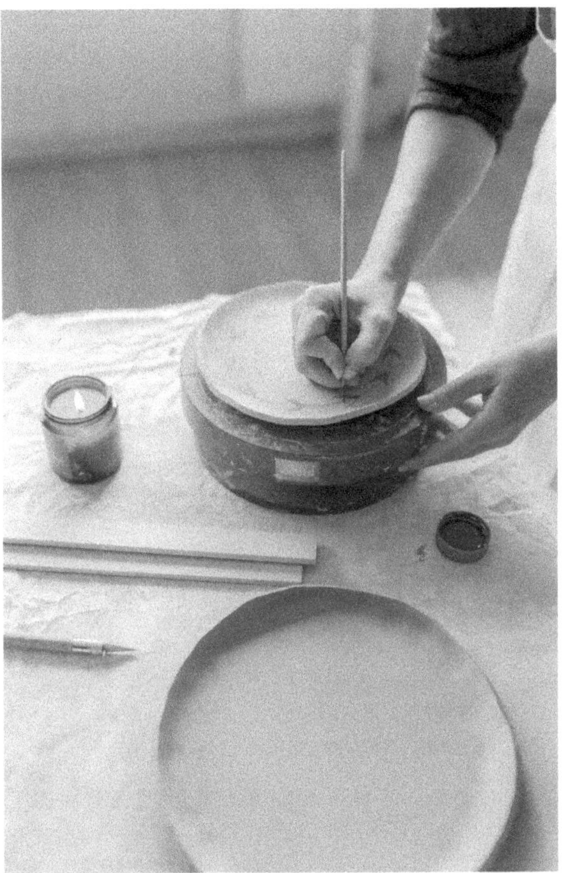

Decorating Greenware

It is possible to carve designs into greenware during its drying process. Additionally, it can be polished using a rough material once it has dried. Although certain greenware pieces may be fired before applying any glaze, you can embellish them with underglazes before their initial bisque firing. Wet greenware can be easily decorated with slips, and the slurry mixture, using coloring agents, can add color and texture.

Different Stages of Drying Clay

Pottery makers utilize several essential terms to characterize the stages of clay drying. It's crucial to be mindful of and comprehend these phases to determine when to connect, proceed with building more significant structures, attach handles, apply slip, engobes, underglaze, and when to abandon the piece.

Unfired clay is referred to as greenware. Once it undergoes its initial firing in the kiln, it transforms into bisque. Bisqueware can be subjected to another glaze firing process or painted using non-firing finishes. During the greenware stage, several drying stages impact the clay's malleability.

Leather-hard

Leather-hard stage is when the piece is stiff, and there is no danger of it getting deformed. But the clay can still be altered, as it is still pliable. This is when potters can carve, use decorative slips, terra sigillata, burnish, smooth, trim, or leave it alone.

Even though clay drying is frequently categorized into distinct phases, it is a continuous process. As the clay dries, it progressively solidifies, leading to various degrees of leather-hard. Clay that has progressed to the leather-hard stage will be more rigid and less pliable, whereas clay still in the initial stages of leather-hardening will be more malleable and easier to manipulate.

The skill in handling clay that has reached the leather-hard stage lies in identifying the appropriate time to ensure that the clay is firm enough to meet your requirements and malleable enough to be shaped. This prompts the query regarding the duration required for clay to attain the leather-hard state.

How long does it take for clay to reach the leather-hard stage?

The clay typically requires 1—3 days to reach the leather-hard stage. Uncovering a newly made pottery piece can accelerate the process to just one day. The duration may be even shorter on a scorching, sunny day.

To dry a pottery piece, wrap it with a plastic sheet. This slows the drying procedure and minimizes the probability of the clay developing cracks during the drying phase.

Cover any embellishments, such as handles, with plastic. Thinner areas of the clay will dry significantly faster than thicker ones. If your pottery dries at different rates, it is more prone to break. Allow the clay to become leather-hard in about 3 days.

Different stages of leather-hard clay

Stage 1: Early Stage

In the initial stage of leather-hard, the clay would still possess a degree of flexibility. You can interact with the clay without it being adhesive or pliant. Nevertheless, you can cautiously handle or manipulate the clay without causing any cracks or harm. Reshaping pottery in this stage is possible because it is pliable.

This phase is ideal for crafting objects such as teapots, cups, or butter dishes, and it's the perfect moment to affix a handle. The clay is at its prime state for making marks and applying a layer of slip to join two parts seamlessly. The optimal time to connect clay is when it has reached a sturdy consistency that is easy to manipulate. Nevertheless, your greenware pieces should also retain enough moisture. The slip will not work as an adhesive if you attempt to connect excessively dry clay pieces.

Tip for joining clay in the leather-hard stage: The pieces that require joining should have a similar moisture content and level. After assembling your leather-hard clay piece, let the pottery rest covered with plastic overnight. The plastic will enable the moisture in the clay pieces and the slip to balance out.

Stage 2: Middle Stage

At this point, the leather-hard clay will have hardened further. You cannot bend the clay without it cracking or breaking. But this stage is good for decorating clay, under glazing, or slipping. At this stage, the clay has enough moisture to allow slipping without cracking. Trimming the clay is also done in this stage.

Stage 3: Third Stage

The last stage of the leather-hard scale is firm leather-hard. At this point in the ceramics process, remove any excess clay that must be smoothed before it reaches the highly delicate bone-dry stage. During the leather-hard stage, I recommend burnishing or embellishing techniques, such as terra sigillata. Trimming, slipping, and carving are not performed at this stage.

As the clay has hardened, potters may burnish their greenware at this stage. Burnishing requires a firm tool to rub the clay in tiny circular motions. Burnishing allows the clay particles to compress, bringing a sheen to the piece's surface.

Tip for the leather-hard stage: The correct level of leather-hardness should be present in your clay. If the clay is too soft, it won't be correctly trimmed, and the handles won't adequately affix to the mug or cup. Cutting and affixing attachments will be challenging if your clay becomes too dry.

Black-hard

Next comes the **Black-hard** stage in drying, when the piece is not soft enough to bear alterations and yet is not completely dry. Little moisture content is still present in the clay, which makes it look dark.

White-hard

White-hard is the phase during the drying of a pottery item when it is thoroughly dry and has minimal moisture. At this juncture, it is prepared to undergo the firing process in the kiln. The item must be as arid as feasible before firing, as any dampness confined within the clay could burst when heated in the kiln.

Bone Dry

The last phase of greenware is when it dries out completely and is ready for firing. At this point, the clay is highly delicate, not malleable, and absorbent. When clay is completely dehydrated before being baked, it is referred to as bone-dry. Despite its solid form, it has a dry texture and is highly delicate. A general guideline is that bone-dry clay will feel room temperature when placed against your skin.

If it is dry, it gives you the feel of room temperature; otherwise, it will feel cool on your skin. Humidity in the air is an essential factor determining the drying time of clay. A pot should dry entirely in one to two weeks in most cases. If a pot dries quicker than that, loosely cover it with plastic. If the pot dries too quickly, it may crack.

The water in the clay travels through the piece to reach its surface to evaporate. However, this may not mean that the piece is completely dried because the deeper layers of the clay may still hold a little moisture. So, it is advisable to wait 2–3 days and allow the piece to be completely dried. Furthermore, the environment in which you live plays a vital role in assisting the clay to reach the bone-dry stage. If you live in a humid climate, there is a good chance that moisture will be present in the deep layers of your clay work.

This is why potters frequently begin their kiln with a preheating phase. When a kiln is preheating, it is drying out the clay rather than firing it. At first, the kiln will need to be warmed gradually to allow sufficient time for the complete evaporation of water. You may quicken the drying process by preheating the pottery in the kiln for a couple of hours at a temperature of 176 °F (80 °C). This phase of the firing, which lasts until the kiln reaches 212 °F (100 °C), is referred to as water smoking, and it facilitates the evaporation of water from the pores between the clay crystals. The preheated state of the kiln is called candling.

A few potters recommend that candling be carried out at a temperature lower than boiling water. The rationale behind this is that when water reaches 212 °F (100 °C), it transforms into steam and expands. This increase in size may lead to the fracturing or bursting of the clay. On the contrary, other potters argue that the water-smoking process needs to be carried out above the boiling point of water because they believe that the remaining water in clay dries out entirely above 212 °F.

Chemically bonded water

Despite the complete evaporation of all moisture in the clay during the candling process, it still retains water. Once the clay is thoroughly dried, its unbound water vaporizes. Nonetheless, the clay particles remain chemically attached to water on a molecular scale. Hence, the kiln should maintain a temperature of 660 °F (384 °C), which allows the clay to dry completely and change to a ceramic state. Once the piece reaches the ceramic state, it is hard and ultimately leaves the stage of workability.

Bisque

The term **"bisque"** can refer to both the firing process and the resulting ceramic piece. This firing process involves subjecting the clay to a temperature that causes a chemical and physical transformation. The water molecules attached to the clay particles burn away, and the particles fuse to create a single, solid piece. Bisqueware is essential in creating glazed ceramics because it allows the piece to absorb the glaze solution, which then adheres to the surface while maintaining the piece's shape. This type of firing is typically considered "low-fire," and some pieces may not be fired at higher temperatures, making them less durable.

Cracking Clay Obstacles

It is highly frustrating to see a clay piece break or crack during the drying stage. When drying, clay can develop cracks if certain areas of the object dry faster than others. As the clay dries, it shrinks, which can create internal tension if some parts of the pottery shrink more quickly than others, consequently leading to cracks.

Though uneven drying is the main reason for cracks, there are a few other factors to consider for why this may be happening.

- Uneven thickness in the wall

Uneven thickness in the pottery wall can lead to uneven drying because thinner areas will dry faster than thicker ones. The moisture in the piece has to travel from the interior to the exterior of the pot, and if the wall is thick, it will require more time, delaying the drying process. This is why mugs and bowls break on the bottom after drying. It's mainly because the piece's base is thicker than the sides. The thinner walls and additions dry faster than the bases.

- Complex designs and details slow the drying process

Ceramics featuring complex patterns are prone to having certain regions that are thinner compared to others. Consequently, the intricacies are prone to drying out faster than the rest of the item. This applies equally to pottery designs that have sharp corners instead of rounded contours. Hence, pots with handles require precise handling while drying is in progress because handles pose a higher risk of breakage.

- Insufficient clay wedging

Proper wedging gives an even consistency to the piece. If the clay has not been wedged thoroughly, it results in dry and dense clay on the one hand and soft clay on the other, with higher water content. So, wedging clay ensures proper moisture distribution throughout the piece to achieve even consistency.

The clay at the base is often less worked-upon compared to the sides. So, there is more possibility of the sides shrinking faster than the base.

- Low-humid weather

The atmosphere in which the clay is crafted is also responsible for its drying. Low-humid levels in the atmosphere lead to rapid drying. Low humidity poses a risk to the uniform drying of your greenware. Placing your ceramics in a breezy location can also result in fissures. The segments of your clay that are exposed to the gust will dry at a faster pace.

- Small cracks in a newly constructed piece

At times, you may notice tiny cracks on freshly crafted edges. This happens because clay has the tendency to dry at thinner edges rapidly. So, the vulnerable points develop small cracks. With the drying process in progress, these tiny cracks can enlarge and pose a higher threat of breakage in the piece.

Steps That Can Combat Cracking

Realizing that your clayware has developed cracks can easily hurt your morale and decrease your motivation. Properly understanding the factors that lead to the development of cracks on the clayware will help you resolve the issue.

- **Try to give an even thickness to your clay**

Try to keep your piece with an even thickness, particularly the bases of mugs, vases, bowls, and cups. A needle tool can aid in checking the thickness of your piece. Insert the pin into the foundation of the ceramics until it reaches the surface of the working table. Afterward, glide your finger along the pin until it reaches the surface of the clay. Now, you may remove the needle to check the distance between your finger and the needle's point to gauge the thickness of your clayware.

- **Keep the pottery covered**

You can control the drying time by covering it with a plastic bag. The layer of plastic ensures that humidity is maintained in the piece. Your surroundings and atmosphere determine whether to seal or leave the piece loosely covered.

Please be aware that moisture may accumulate on the inner side of the plastic bag. The bag may meet the clay surface, making the clay damp and imprinting on your pottery.

I recommend shielding your pottery with non-waxed newspaper to prevent this from happening. Non-waxed newspaper will soak up any humidity from the bag and prevent it from adhering to your pottery.

- **Prevent pottery cracking by storing the piece in a damp box**

You can use a wet box to cover your pottery. A damp box may be readily made by laying a 1–2-inch layer of plaster in the plastic box. When the plaster has hardened, you can add water to make it more or less moist. Put your newly crafted piece inside the damp box and cover it with a lid. The inside of the box should provide an air-free damp environment to the piece and initiate the drying process. You have complete control by maintaining the inside temperature of the box; you may add more water to the plaster to create humidity inside, or you may leave the lid open to allow air drying.

An alternative method for addressing cracked handles on mugs during the clay drying is to moisten your greenware again. A damp box is an effective means of evenly rehydrating pots and mugs.

The plaster inside the damp box must be damp, but not to the extent that the greenware is submerged in water. Water in the plaster helps maintain a moist environment in the container and rehydrates dry clay gradually.

After rehydrating the fractured object, you can reconnect the handle by applying a slip. When the piece's body and handle share an equal moisture level, the chances of breakage are bleak.

If your pottery base is thick, consider putting the pot inside the damp box. The plaster will absorb moisture from the piece and allow even drying of the clayware.

- **Turn your clayware to save it from cracking**

After your ceramic is firm enough to lift without causing any harm, you can flip it. This is advantageous as it allows air to reach the lower part.

- **Put your pottery on a shelf or rack**

As stated earlier, I advise placing your finished piece on a wire rack or shelf to initiate even drying so that air reaches all sides of the piece. A well-ventilated area is considered ideal for placing the pottery for drying because air circulates on all sides, ensuring even drying of the piece.

- **Ensure that the pieces are perfectly joined**

To ensure the proper bonding of two ceramic pieces, the most effective method is to score and slip (please refer to adhesion methods in Chapter 8).

Why Do Mug Handles Crack Upon Drying?

Handles tend to dry faster than the rest of the piece because they are usually thinner, and air circulation surrounds them. The difference in moisture content between the mug and the handle is uneven, leading to cracks when the piece dries. Sometimes, potters attach handles to a dried piece without realizing it is too late for the handle to stay firmly on the clayware.

Here are a few tips to ensure the handles are securely bonded to a piece and significantly reduce the chances of cracking.

Use vinegar or vinegar slurry

Take a minute quantity of bone-dry clay. The amount of mud required will vary according to the magnitude of the crack. However, generally, a portion equivalent to the size of a tomato should suffice.

Use the similar type of mud that you've used to fashion your cups. Pound the withered mud into fragments using a spoon, mortar, and pestle. Make a powder of bone-dry clay.

Pour a small quantity of vinegar into the powdered clay to make a thick paste. Vinegar acts as a flocculant, causing clay fragments to stick together. It thickens clay slurries.

Dab some vinegar on the split joint with a sponge before applying the paste. Avoid getting the clay near the fracture too damp. It would help if you moistened it. If you make it overly moist, you create another drying gradient.

Now, apply some vinegar paste to the crack. Put the paste inside the seam using a modeling or a wooden tool, then smooth the surface. Allow the filling to dry, and most likely, it will develop a crack again.

Repeat the entire process and keep doing it until the crack stays fully closed upon drying.

Wrap the handle with a cloth or paper towel

An alternative method for restoring moisture to unfired clay is to ensure it is in a dampened, smooth-textured fabric and seal it within a plastic enclosure. I recommend using a lightweight fabric to minimize the risk of any imprints transferring to the clay surface. You can use damp towels that shall help to keep the piece moistened. But you must be careful and keep an eye on the towel because if the towel dries, the piece will also dry. So, if required, occasionally moisten the towel so that the clayware remains damp.

Once the piece is evenly moist, you may use the score-and-slip method to attach the handle again.

Once the pottery is completely dried and ready for the first firing process, it is ready for the first firing. In the following chapter, we will go over the first firing stage of dried clayware.

10

FIRST FIRING STAGE

Having sound knowledge about the firing process of ceramics can guarantee good results in pottery. Firing adds durability and strength to your piece. When clay is fired, it undergoes a chemical transformation that makes it stronger and more durable, a process known as vitrification.

Pottery involves the firing of work twice, namely bisque firing followed by glaze firing. The objective of bisque firing is to transform greenware into a robust, partially vitrified permeable state that can be handled securely while glazing and embellishing. Additionally, it eliminates carbonaceous substances (organic matter present in clay, paper, etc.).

What Happens to Clay in the Firing Process?

When the clay enters the kiln, it undergoes physical changes. The water content is evaporated from the clay. The potter has to ensure that the pottery is completely dry because as it gets heated, the released steam may cause an explosion. The best method is to heat the kiln slowly so that the water completely evaporates. Preheating the clayware in the kiln for a few hours at 176 °F (80 °C) will speed up drying. The firing temperature can reach up to 212 °F (100 °C), causing water evaporation within the pores of clay crystals; this process is called water smoking.

If the kiln is cooled rapidly by opening it too soon, some areas of the ware may be stressed due to the sudden contraction of cristobalite by 3% at 439 °F (226 °C), leading to cracking. I recommend waiting until the temperature drops below 212 °F (100 °C) before opening the kiln and cooling it down to prevent cracking. This gradual cooling procedure is identified as annealing, which guarantees the durability of the clay and minimizes the chances of cracking while being used.

Different Types of Clay Require Different Temperature Treatments

The firing process commences when the pottery items are set at high temperatures in a kiln. This temperature fluctuates based on the type of clay and the intended effects. Earthenware is a low-fire clay and is usually burned at temperatures ranging from 1,800 °F to 2,200 °F, whereas stoneware is fired at higher temperatures ranging between 2,200 °F to 2,600 °F.

In general, the influence of fire on clay can be considerable, depending upon the clay variety, the degree of heat exposure, and the ensuing chemical reactions. Clay subjected to higher temperatures during firing may become brittle and sensitive to breakage, whereas clay fired at lower temperatures may become sturdier. Furthermore, smoke and chemical reactions can impact the clay.

Different Methods of Firing and Their Impact

Diverse techniques of firing ceramics can help attain distinct hues and textures on your pottery creations.

Oxidation and Reduction

Oxidative firing occurs when an abundant amount of oxygen is present in the kiln during the firing process. Throughout this procedure, the oxygen particles adhere to the pottery and interact with the glaze and the clay surface. As the item is fired, the oxygen possesses a high level of electronegativity, drawing electrons from the glaze and clay, leading to their oxidation.

Reduction firing occurs when the kiln's oxygen supply is limited. As a result, various gases, including carbon, hydrogen, and carbon dioxide, accumulate in the kiln. This transforms the oxides in the kiln and clay, ultimately modifying the appearance and consistency of your pottery creations.

Kilns and the Styles that Impact Firing Results

Different firing techniques yield different results on clayware. Clay pieces tend to acquire a distinct appearance due to the firing techniques.

- Electric Kilns

The most popular method of firing pottery is in electric kilns. They are generally affordable and equipped with user-friendly digital controls. The interior of electric kilns is typically lined with insulating bricks and can be loaded either from the top or front, depending on the model.

The coils that wrap the pottery heat up to fire it, ensuring the components within are equally heated. Electric kilns are dependable and easy to operate, especially since you can program the kiln to fire your works on a timetable.

- Gas Kilns

Some potters prefer gas kilns, although they are less prevalent than electric kilns. They can facilitate salt or soda firing, resulting in diverse textures and hues compared to those produced in an electric kiln. The flames within the kiln can be regulated to modify the environment inside, altering the appearance and tactile qualities of your ceramic creations.

- Wood-Burning Kilns

Wood-burning Kilns are the oldest method of firing clay and are less prevalent in modern times. These are manufactured by the potters with bricks and look like igloos. But the process is manual, time-consuming, and labor-intensive. But it is one of the most organic techniques that give the clay piece a beautiful and rustic look.

Methods of firing

After becoming familiar with the different types of kilns, take note of these other firing methods:

- Soda Firing

When baking soda and sodium carbonate are placed within the kiln having a temperature of 2,350 °F, these vaporize and disperse inside the kiln. The vapor sticks to the pottery within the kiln to give a glaze-like impact on the surface of the clay body.

- Raku Firing

Raku firing is a process where the pottery is taken out of the kiln while it's still red-hot. Afterward, it's put inside a container with either paper or sawdust, which will ignite, producing an atmosphere with reduced oxygen that can lead to unexpected yet exceptional outcomes. There are various ways to finish the cooling process, which may result in a distinctive crackle pattern on the final product. Every single one of these coarse, natural designs is distinct.

- Sawdust Firing

This type of firing is done in a DIY kiln. The sawdust is placed inside the kiln, and the item is installed on the sawdust, and the top of the part is also covered with dust. The firing happens slowly and can take up to 36 hours to achieve excellent results.

Firing should be a slow and gradual process. Why?

It is highly significant to allow clayware to dry completely. Larger pieces should be given more time to dry so that the inner layers have enough time to lose moisture. Drying wet clay that is moistened with water involves air-drying. As the clay begins to dry, the water dissipates. This causes the clay particles to move closer together, leading to shrinkage. Inconsistent drying rates that generate tension in the clay are responsible for various issues with clay—the clay's tension results in the development of cracks in the piece during or after the firing stage. So, ensure even dryness; you already know how to achieve even drying in clayware.

Shrinkage

The reduction in clay size during firing is due to various factors. Firstly, it experiences a loss of moisture. Secondly, it undergoes both physical and chemical transformations that lead to an increased density compared to its initial state. The degree of shrinkage during drying and firing varies depending on the type of clay used, which can range from 4% to as much as 15%. Clay typically contains about 20% water and 9% organic matter, resulting in a final weight reduction of up to 30%.

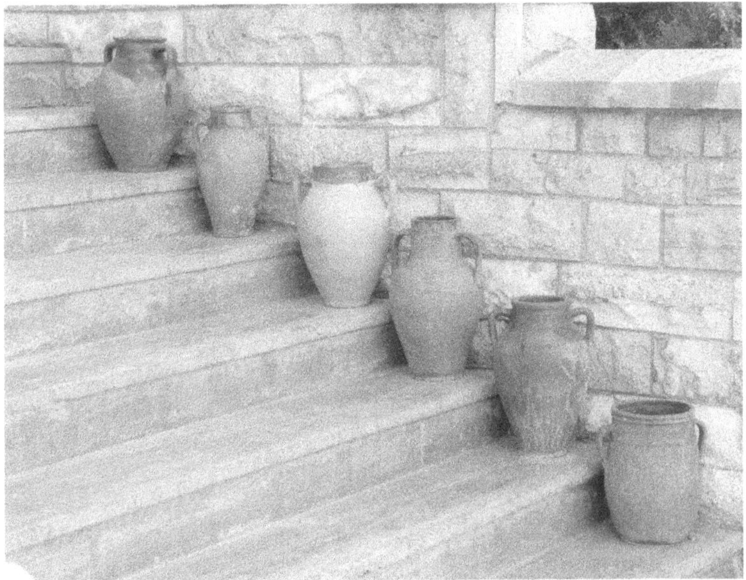

Bisque Stage: Understanding Glazes

Glazing and firing are significant pottery stages; if you are a beginner, which comes first?

So, glazing comes after the first firing stage. The first firing stage is called bisque firing, and this makes the clayware permanently acquire hardness and shape, but still, the clay is porous enough to undergo glazing. Glazes and underglazes are applied on bisque-fired clayware, followed by a second firing.

The second round of firing clay is referred to as the glaze firing. Once the bisque firing is completed, a liquid glaze is added to the pottery. It is then subjected to a second firing, causing the glaze to liquefy and create a smooth glassy coating on the pottery.

Firing and Glazing

What Is Glazing in Pottery?

Glazes consist of finely pulverized minerals in a liquid form that can be applied to pottery using a brush, pour, or dip technique. After the glaze layers have dried, the pottery is carefully loaded into a kiln and heated to the temperature required for the glaze to fuse with the clay and create a glossy finish and vibrant and unique colors.

Glazing is fun because it adorns your clayware and turns it into a stunning piece. Glazes are available in different colors. To add the glaze onto the bisque ware, use a brush, sponge, or spray gun, and pour or immerse the complete piece into a glazed pool.

When you're satisfied with your glazing results, allow the piece to dry completely before putting it in the kiln for the glaze firing. The glaze firing process ensures that the glaze attains the ideal melting point. Similar to the bisque firing process, it is important to attain the correct temperature to prevent the glaze from cracking.

Tips for Glaze Firing

- Ensure your pottery stays clean after the bisque-firing process. Additionally, I recommend using disposable or rubber gloves while handling the items to prevent the formation of resist spots caused by lotions and oils from your hands.
- Before glaze firing, ensure the piece is free from rough spots

you may have missed during bisque firing. Wet sandpaper
can provide a smooth texture to your clay piece.

- Ensure proper mixing and straining of glaze before
applying it on the surface of bisque ware.

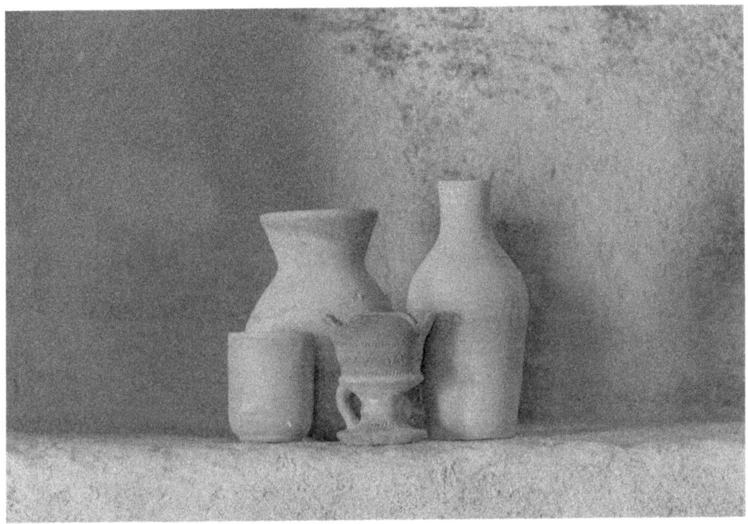

- Lastly, but most importantly, check the dryness of the glaze
before placing your piece in the kiln for the second firing.

What should you do if you want to fire your piece only once?

Although most potters prefer firing their clay pieces twice, it is
feasible to forego the two-step firing process and opt for a single-
firing technique. In this case, the glazing is applied to the surface of
the unfired clay, at the bone-dry stage of your greenware. Skilled
potters who create their own glazes usually employ this approach,
ensuring they are tailored to work well with a single firing. It's essential to remember that not all glazes are compatible with this method,
as most commercial glazes are formulated for a bisque firing initially.
When using a single-firing method, the organic matter in the clay
has yet to be burnt off, which can result in errors during the firing
process.

Single-firing your clay piece can be challenging due to the increased risk of errors. The glazing process may result in issues like crawling and pin-holing. Nonetheless, a few skilled potters have perfected this technique. It is feasible to attain superb ceramic embellishments even with a one-step firing. Check out the benefits of single and double firing before taking the important step ahead.

There are benefits to consider for both single firing and double firing:

Single-Firing

- It is time-efficient and less laborious.
- It saves energy and is more economical to fire just once.
- Even if you have underglazed your greenware, it remains intact after a single firing.

Double Firing

- It guarantees that carbon-containing substances are combusted during the initial firing to prevent any impact on the glazes, thereby assuring an improved end outcome.
- Applying glazes on a bisque-fired piece is much quicker and simpler because it is less sensitive and fragile.
- Errors that you make while glazing are easy to rectify.
- It is a superior option for ceramists who favor ornamental methods such as 'glaze elimination.' For instance, you can eliminate the elevated areas of a textured glaze by wiping them off.

Understanding Glazes

Having a sound knowledge of glazes and their application makes the potter's journey of mastering the craft simpler and more attractive in multiple ways. Using glaze on ceramics primarily aims to render them waterproof and safe for storing food. Ceramics made of clay, fired once, are neither waterproof nor safe for storing food until they are coated with glaze and fired again. Here are a couple of facts related to glazes.

Choosing Your Glaze

Buying the right glaze can be confusing if you are unaware of the factors you need to consider to make the right buying decision. Follow the steps mentioned below to bring the right glaze for your ceramics.

What should you look for in a pottery glaze?

- Low firing temperature

I advise searching for glazes that can be heated at a lower temperature. The temperature range for such glazes should ideally be between 1700 °F to 2000 °F. The low-heat coating produces vibrant hues, is cost-effective, and is extensively used in the ceramic industry because of its desired outcomes.

- Toxic-free

Glazes should be toxic-free because these are used as coatings on ceramics designed to store food. So, check the label before buying; it should be toxin and lead-free.

Ensure that the glaze you use for creating your ceramics has minimal lead proportion. The finished piece's considerable amount of lead can lead to viral health problems or food contamination.

- Ingredients

Most ceramic glazes are composed of essential elements unless elaborate, such as those with a crackle or matte finish. All ceramic glazes have four primary constituents: flux, silica, alumina, and colorant. These constituents blend to create a glassy texture, a steady melting point, and a vividly colored layer when the glaze is applied to the ceramic.

Which type should you buy?

- Tinted glaze

Tinted glazes contain added colors and have gained popularity among potters of all levels, from amateurs to experts. Using these glazes saves time, as there is no need to apply pottery paint and then coat it with a clear glaze.

- Opaque glaze

The opaque glaze is renowned for the consistency it produces. Compared to other coatings, the non-transparent glaze doesn't provide a vivid shine to the ceramic exterior. Instead, it makes subtle touches of shine in specific areas while providing an overall matte finish.

- Transparent glaze

These are the original and oldest forms of glaze invented in the relevant field. It gives a shine to the surface color to obtain a glass-like finish. The translucent glaze gives a foggy finish and slightly changes the underneath color.

- Matte glaze

A matte glaze is devoid of gloss or shine. It eliminates the luster of the pottery coating and imparts an exceptionally smooth but dry appearance. Matte glazes are obtainable in various hues, and the upshot is identical to that of employing a lucid matte glaze.

- Textured glaze

The coating of patterns in pottery is done with a textured glaze. The design appears authentic; however, it's only an illusion coated in shine upon contact. There are numerous textured coatings, such as marble coating, shattered glass coating, and melted texture coating.

Techniques for Glazing Pottery

If you want to obtain practical and foolproof glazing results, I advise following these steps and techniques.

Dipping Technique

If you are a beginner with glazing, then the dipping technique is the best way to begin. Sieve the glaze to acquire a fine and smooth-textured result. Dipping, primarily, is helpful in two ways—firstly, it can be used as a base layer application just before any adornment. After the final decoration, You must dip the piece into the glaze again.

Secondly, it can be used as a solid decoration in pieces without adornment. Start by blending the glaze adequately. Subsequently, strain it and persistently blend it to form a uniform mixture. Afterward, based on the desired texture, you can ascertain the thickness.

Identify the strong part of the ceramic item and grasp it using tongs. Immerse it into the glaze, ensuring you're securely holding it. As you submerge the artwork into the glaze solution, proceed slowly to avoid the formation of bubbles or splatters. Allow the piece to sit in the glaze for 3 to 5 seconds before lifting it vertically. Shake the piece gently to get rid of excess glaze. Remove tong or any other marks on the surface of your piece with a soft brush and even it out.

Dripping/Pouring Technique

Dripping is commonly linked with embellishing the ceramic item while pouring. Dripping and pouring have identical meanings. The pouring method is categorized into two segments. Initially, the crucial aspect is accomplishing a base through the pouring procedure. Pour the glaze on your piece and allow it to sit for 4–5 seconds. Pour the excess glaze back into the bucket. Your piece must have a uniform glaze over it by now.

It's necessary to conceal the outer surface of the ceramic piece. Elevate your creation above a petite dish and start pouring the glaze into a design of your liking. You can conceal the complete article to generate a pouring design if you desire. Artisans can eliminate any surplus glaze by using a gentle sponge or cotton swabs to attain smoothness.

Afterward, opt for a colored coating that differs from the underlying shade. Transfer it into a flexible container. Squeeze the container along the circumference of the vase. Dispense an ample amount so that the coating runs down to the bottom of the object from all sides due to the force of gravity. The act of dripping produces a stunning effect, particularly when contrasting hues are employed.

Brushing Technique

The brushing technique is excellent for decoration and base layer glazing. The brushing technique applies to both greenware and bisque ware. However, it can be tricky for greenware because the natural components present in the greenware have yet to undergo combustion, which may lead to specific problems.

Spraying Technique

Spraying is most effective for applying the initial layer of glaze. However, compared to other glazing methods, it can make designing more challenging, as it does not produce the most delicate textures.

Splattering Technique

A stiff brush is helpful for the splattering technique. One of the most effective methods to embellish pottery items is employing a foundation coating using spattering and then complementing it with spatters of varying hues. Vivid shades will appear stunning on an unadorned white foundation. Dark spatters will appear fantastic on solid bases of red, white, yellow, and green.

Stippling Technique

When stippling, apply the glaze using a gentle brush and its pointed end. One of the most favored methods in stippling is to gather a tiny quantity of glaze at the brush tip. Ensure you use the minimum amount of product and avoid overloading it, as it disturbs the texture.

Sponging Technique

Use natural or synthetic sponges to get interesting glazing results. The remarkable absorbency of sponges expedites the pottery glazing procedure. I recommend using synthetic sponges, which can be trimmed into specific shapes or patterns, unlike natural sponges.

Elaborate designs are produced by delicate sponges with a fine texture, whereas sturdy, coarse, and sizable sponges aid in covering a broader area. Furthermore, they are highly efficient in establishing the base layer of pottery.

Glaze Trailing Technique

Glaze trailing is the technique for you if you want to create natural and abstract artwork on your pottery. The versatility of the method is that it is applicable on both glazed as well as clay bases. The technique utilizes a small, squeezable container with a nozzle end known as the slip dispenser. Merely submerge the implement into the glaze or saturate it entirely and commence designing the pattern. In glaze trailing, the lines will melt. To master the skill, becoming an expert in the technique would be very handy, as it can be slightly tricky for beginners.

Wax Resist With Glaze Technique

Wax resist repels glazes; hence glaze will not adhere to the spots where wax resist is applied. So, the trick is to use the wax resist on your pottery first. Then allow the wax to dry before applying the glaze to the piece. Let the piece dry again, and wipe the extra glaze using a sponge.

The wax resist technique removes the glaze from specific areas of the pottery. It can also protect a glazed surface from additional coatings of glaze. Applying wax resist to the bottom of the pottery can prevent the unwanted glaze. This technique allows for creativity and the showcasing of skills.

Mocha Diffusion Technique

The mocha diffusion technique is a glazing method that perfectly finishes your artwork. It creates tree-like patterns or organic veins. To begin, coat the area and create a mixture of cider vinegar and mason stain. Apply the mixture over the slip with a paintbrush, and once the vinegar touches the slip, the spread will begin.

Though all the different techniques do not apply to all potters, they can try their hand at experimenting with artistic ways of glazing and master the technique which thrills and excites them. Undoubtedly, glazing produces impressive results.

11

SETTING EXPECTATIONS FOR THE SECOND FIRING

Glazing in pottery can add a beautiful finish to your work, but it's important to be aware of potential defects and hazards that can arise from improper glazing. Imperfections such as pinholes, crawling, blistering, and crazing can occur and pose health hazards. However, these defects can also result in unique and visually striking patterns, adding an aesthetic element to your work. By understanding the common glazing defects, we'll also go over how to address these so that you can create safe and beautiful pottery.

Glazing Defects

Glazing can be tricky if you are unaware of the defects that may shock or surprise you. You will be astonished to know that some potters deliberately do faulty glazing because they like to create an aesthetic appearance in their art pieces. In this chapter, you will become acquainted with the different defects in glazing so that you may quickly identify the flaw to prevent the issue from happening with your next masterpiece.

Significant glazing defects are outlined in this chapter for a better understanding of the subject.

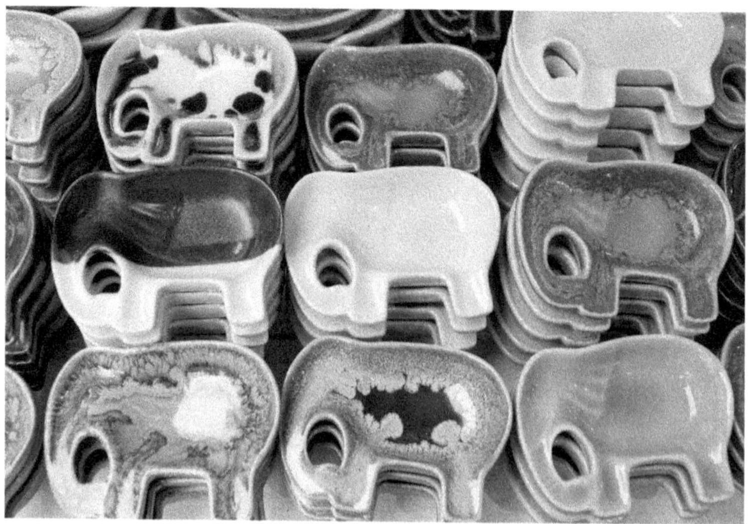

Crazing

If the glaze undergoes more significant shrinkage than the clay material during cooling, it will result in a glaze-cracked defect called crazing. It is one of the most common glazing defects and is simple to correct too. It leads to the development of lines in your pottery's fired and glazed surface. Craze lines may trap particles (such as food, dust, or dirt) and foster bacterial growth, rendering them unsuitable for food use. Crazing can be corrected with the help of the following measures.

- Crazing can frequently be eradicated just by administering a thin glaze layer. Although a thin layer is not feasible in some instances, a minor reduction in glaze thickness will often halt crazing.
- Increase the amount of flint in the formula without modifying the proportions of the other elements. Use a fine mesh. Incorporate 200 mesh flints into the clay mixture. Gradually enhance the flint proportion by 5%, 10%, and 15%.
- Bake the ceramic to the appropriate cone for an extended duration in the glaze kiln. Aim to fire the piece one or two cones higher without adversely impacting the clayware.

- Gradually lower the temperature of the glaze kiln. Avoid opening the door until the temperature drops below 390 °F (200 °C).

How does crazing impact food safety?

Lead Crazing

Before consuming meals on pottery plates, it is imperative to exercise vigilance toward safety. The FDA in the United States monitors the precise levels of cadmium and lead present in pottery, ensuring that each piece is free from these harmful substances. The process of leaching is employed to determine the food safety of dishware. There is a genuine worry regarding the release of lead into food and beverages from pottery baked using lead glazes.

Sour fluids are especially noteworthy. Likewise, sustained microwave warming (for instance, a workplace cup of coffee) may increase lead coatings' leaching. Although commercial ceramics firms frequently examine their products for lead leakage, artisanal potters need comparable quality assurance, resulting in a greater risk of lead leakage.

Other Leachable Metals

Additional metals have the potential to infiltrate food and beverages. In the United States and Canada, cadmium is the only metal alongside lead that's currently restricted. However, other harmful metals found in glazes can seep into food. It is advisable to opt for glazes that contain calcium, magnesium, potassium, and sodium fluxes and limit the use of toxic metal colorants. It is necessary to conduct regular assessments to detect the leaching of other metals.

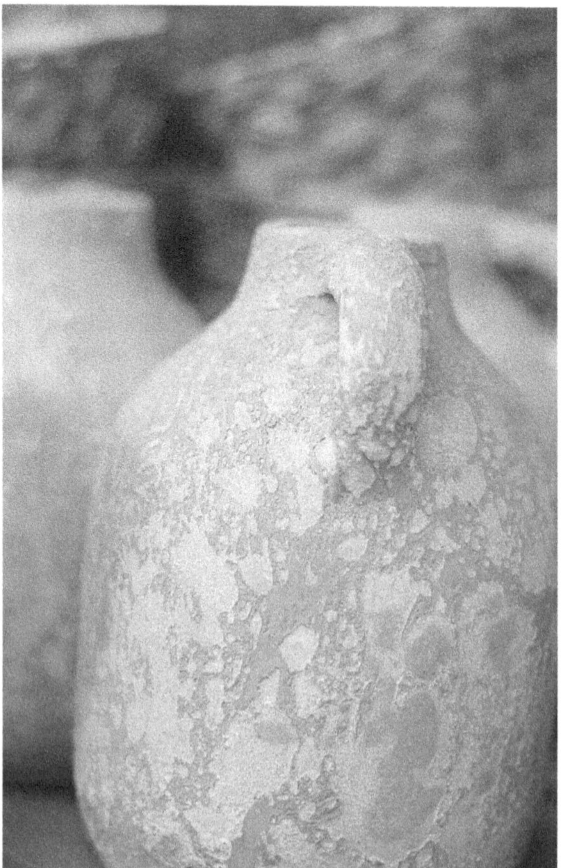

Shivering

Shivering defects happen when the clay material undergoes more significant shrinkage than the glaze while cooling. Shivering occurs when fragments of glaze strip, fracture, or peel break away from the edges of pottery. On occasions, the bits of enamel or underglaze are tiny and extremely sharp. This phenomenon arises due to the contradiction in the thermal expansion of the clay body and the glaze or underglaze (for instance, the bisque and glaze expand or shrink at different rates).

Despite being categorized as a glaze imperfection, shivering can be rectified by modifying the glaze formula, the clay body formula, or both. Shivering can be triggered by clay bodies that possess excessive free silica, and fireclays tend to have irregularly high levels of free silica. Additionally, using fine grog containing a high concentration of silica can lead to shivering, especially if it has been burned onto the clay surface during the forming stage.

Here are the practical steps to prevent shivering:

- In case a single glaze is experiencing shivering on the clay body, attempt incorporating 5, 10, or 15 units of potash feldspar into that particular glaze.
- Modifying the flint content in a glaze by reducing it by 5 or 10 units can effectively regulate the compatibility between the clay body and the glaze.
- In some cases, the inclusion of feldspar/frit and the exclusion of flint may help to prevent shivering.
- To resolve the issue of multiple glazes shivering on the same body, incorporate 5, 10, or 15 parts of feldspar (or other alkali-bearing materials) into the clay formula.
- The reduction of flint by 5 or 10 units in the clay body can also rectify glaze shivering.

Generally, shivering in the glaze can be rectified by incorporating feldspar, frit, or other materials with high expansion. If the issue persists, the remedy is to modify the clay body recipe or switch to a different clay body altogether.

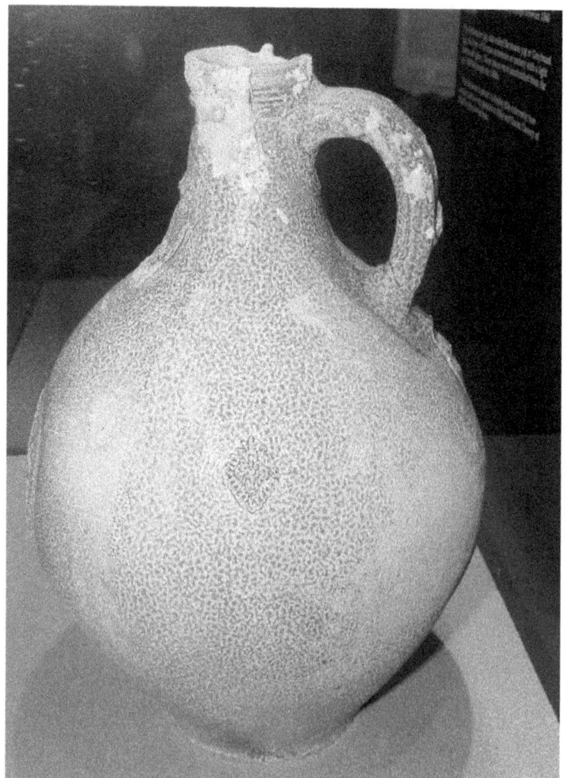

Crawling

The crawling defect is due to high surface tension within the glaze as its melting. This issue is commonly caused by poor application, leading to adhesion problems. It typically appears in areas where the glaze is excessively powdery and fails to adhere to the clay's surface. Adding a small amount of gum to the glaze mixture can help eliminate this problem. Crawling is more prevalent in matte glazes than in fluid ones, but sometimes adding a small amount of extra flux can reduce the crawling issue.

Furthermore, applying one glaze over another, especially if the first one dries out entirely before the second application, can cause crawling. Certain fluxes, such as zinc and magnesium, are likely to cause crawling when used excessively. Calcining some or all the zinc can help alleviate this issue.

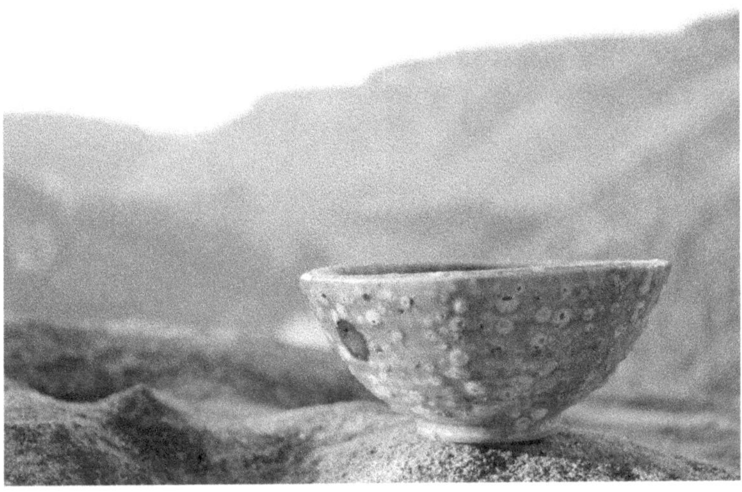

Pitting and Pinholing

These are the most bothersome and challenging glaze imperfections to deal with. They may result from an inadequately managed firing schedule and the glaze formulation or may stem from the clay body, especially those with a high proportion of grog.

To reduce them, you may employ smaller particles, increase the flux quantity, put on a secondary, thinner glaze coating, and utilize a kiln with proper ventilation. You may even increase the maturing temperature of the kiln to rectify the issue.

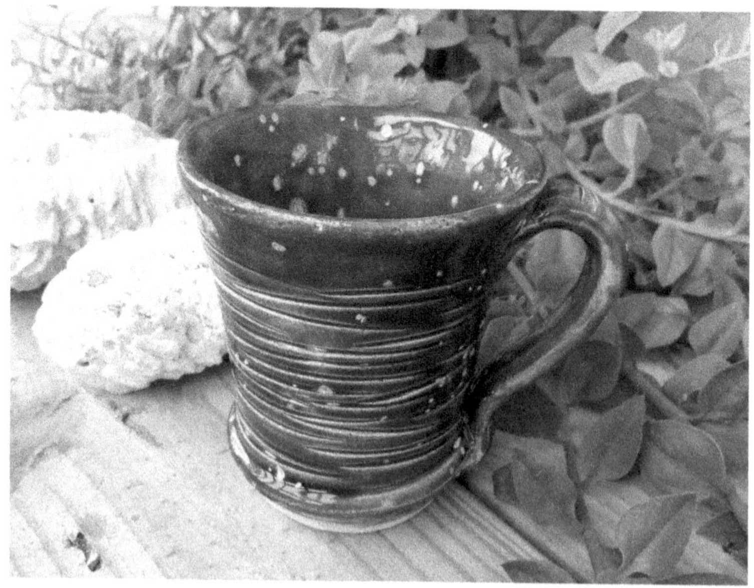

Blistering

As the name suggests, these look like craters found on the moon's surface. These are found in fired glaze surfaces with sharp or soft round edges. These appear in the final stage of firing or the initial cooling phase. These may vary in size and appear more prominent if the glaze is thick and uneven.

The presence of fluxes in the glaze, like boric acid, magnesium sulfate, sodium carbonate, or potassium carbonate, can cause the problem. Replacing these items with other fluxing mediums or fritted agents is better.

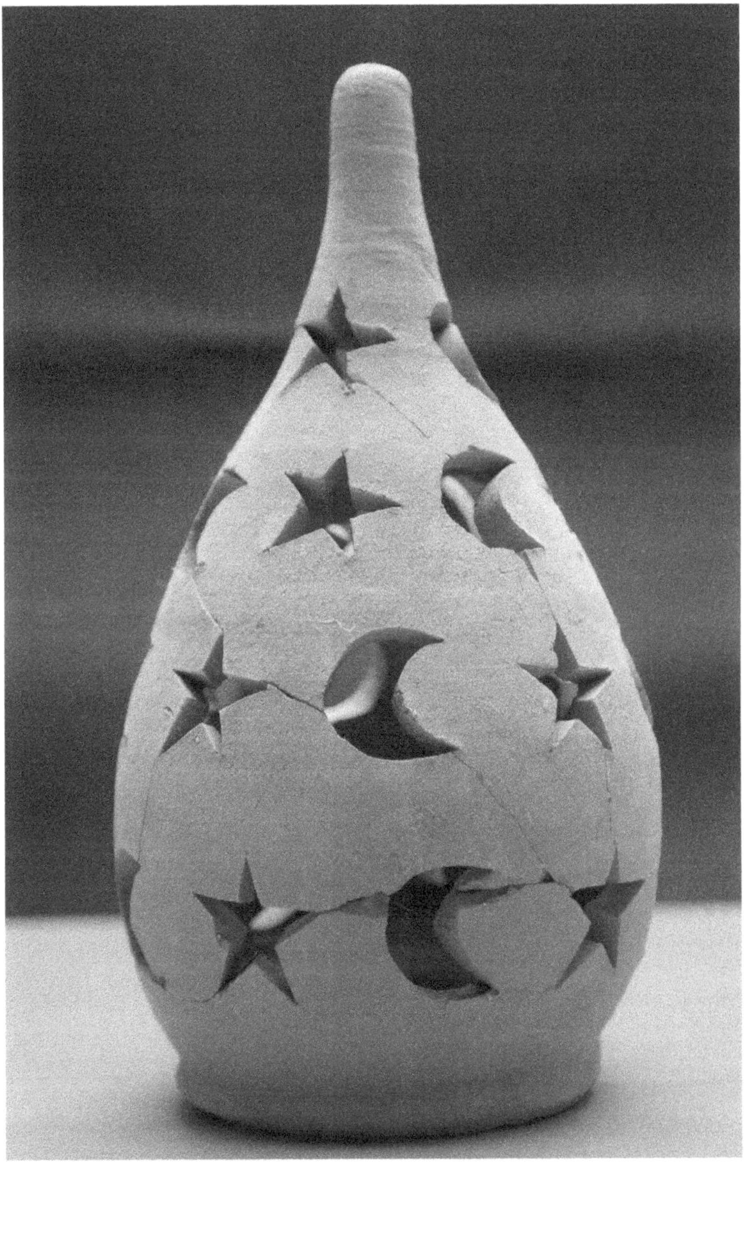

Dunting

Dunting is a crack that develops due to pressures induced by firing and cooling. These pressures are generated mainly during two crucial times of firing known as silica inversions, which occur around 1063 °F (573 °C) and 439 °F (226 °C). During these points of inversion, the arrangement of the silica molecules undergoes a structural reorganization. It is crucial to fire the material gradually through these two temperatures, and electronic kiln profiles are often programmed to do this automatically while heating.

The most intimidating aspect, however, is induced during the cooling process. These fractures manifest as lengthy, distinct, structural cracks with precise boundaries. The glaze has sharp edges if the ceramic is coated with a glaze. These fractures can take on a vertical, horizontal, or spiral pattern. Three reasons are responsible for dunts while cooling.

1. Firstly, it happens when the temperature drops below 1063 °F (573 °C) and the first silica inversion takes place. During this inversion, the clay piece undergoes an abrupt contraction. The degree of contraction is directly proportional to the amount of silica, or quartz, present in the structure. However, since different sections of the vessel cool at varying rates, there is no uniform contraction, resulting in internal stresses that can lead to cracking. Consider a tall vessel, for instance. The upper portion will cool more quickly than the lower portion, which is insulated by the kiln shelf. As a result, the upper section will contract faster than the lower section, leading to a crack along the bottom of the wall.

2. The second happens when you cool through the 439 °F inversion. A similar situation occurs as described above. However, potters occasionally prefer to open their kilns around this temperature to inspect their work, which might exacerbate the problem.

3. The third variety of cooling failure occurs several months or even years after firing. For instance, a vessel may divide into two halves after three months. This is possibly due to thermal shock. In such situations, the clay and glaze expand at different rates when subjected to temperature fluctuations, resulting in a fracture. To put it more precisely,

the clay body contracts more than the glaze. The glaze will shatter (as previously mentioned) if it is less robust. If the clay is more robust, the object will stay intact.

Remember that most fractures transpire during the drying stages, though they may become visible much later. Nonetheless, certain fractures arise due to heating and chilling; therefore, I recommend carrying out this process gradually.

CONCLUSION

Throughout this journey, we have acknowledged the frustrations and limitations that can accompany the pursuit of hand-building pottery. We are fortunate to use a reserve of information that is persistently expanding with new trials and technological progressions. However, I have also shared remarkable solutions and techniques to help you overcome these challenges and advance your pottery skills.

The step-by-step guidance for creating different clay projects outlined in the book helps you understand versatile pottery design techniques. It serves as one of the best guides for beginners since it is packed with informative and practical insights about the different methods of hand-building clay.

The art of pottery-making by hand is an excellent approach to enhancing pottery skills. Applying this knowledge will elevate the worth of your craftsmanship and produce far more significant masterpieces.

Though you may consider learning pottery to escape a mundane lifestyle, you may even transform your passion into your profession!

Remember, pottery is not just a craft; it is a form of expression that allows you to disconnect from the world's distractions and fully immerse yourself in the world of pottery. It provides therapeutic benefits, a space for personal growth, and time to decompress. It remains a timeless art form cherished by artists like yourself who appreciate beautiful and extraordinary art.

As we reach the end of this journey, I want to extend my gratitude for embarking on this path of creative exploration. May your pottery endeavors continue to bring you immense satisfaction and fulfillment. With the techniques and shortcuts you've learned, may you craft remarkable ceramics that leave a lasting impression on yourself and those who have the privilege to admire your creations.

I wish you all the very best in your future pottery endeavors. I trust this book has provided invaluable assistance in this pursuit. May your artistic journey be filled with endless inspiration, profound growth, and an ever-expanding passion for the world of hand-building pottery.

REVIEW REQUEST

Hello there, esteemed pottery artists!

If you've already embarked on this creative journey through Hand-Building Pottery, I'd love to hear about your experiences by sharing your thoughts in leaving an honest review.

Your journey and experiences in pottery are incredibly valuable – they hold the power to inspire and encourage others to dive headfirst into the beautiful world of hand-building pottery! Imagine a newcomer to pottery, flipping through countless books, unsure which one to choose. Your review can be their compass, pointing them directly to this book's treasure trove of knowledge.

Your review and honest thoughts on "Hand Building Pottery" can be the guiding light for fellow art enthusiasts, helping them find a book that truly speaks to their creative souls. Your distinctive viewpoint can spark someone else's passion for pottery or even inspire them to elevate their ceramic skills to heights amidst a delightful mess of clay and boundless artistic potential! Your review will also motivate and encourage me to continue creating exceptional content that nurtures the creative spirit of countless readers.

If you've enjoyed this book, please take a moment, and leave an honest review for "Hand Building Pottery." It's as easy as adding glaze to a finished piece! If you purchased the book online, head to the platform where you made the magic happen – whether it's Amazon, Goodreads, or any other online bookstore.

To leave a review on Amazon, scan this QR code:

From there, you can rate the book and share your thoughts. Your heartfelt reviews will not only rock the pottery world, but will also leave a lasting impact on aspiring potters and beginners alike. So, thank you from the bottom of my heart, your support means the world to me, and I can't wait to see your reviews brightening up the pottery world!

Thank you for being a part of this fantastic pottery adventure.

Happy creating, and may your artistic endeavors be filled with joy and inspiration!

GLOSSARY

Burnishing: A method of smoothing leather-hard or black-hard clay by rubbing it with a hard smooth item such as a stone, spoon, or piece of glass. This process gives the object a polished appearance.

Calcining: Heating a solid chemical substance to high temperatures without melting it while limiting the amount of available oxygen in the environment to remove impurities.

Greenware: Stage when pottery has not been fired.

Deflocculant: A substance included in slip to enhance its flow properties.

Grog: Ground, unglazed ceramics or bricks are utilized as a supplement in plaster or clay.

Impermeable: Fluid that is not allowed to pass.

Kaolin: Also called China Clay; is used for making porcelain.

Kiln: A furnace for firing and burning pottery.

Sintered: Sintering, also known as frittage, is the process of compacting and producing a solid mass of material using pressure or heat without melting it completely. Sintering is a manufacturing method that is utilized with metals, ceramics, polymers, and other substances.

Slab Rollers: An automated or hand-operated apparatus for flattening sizable consistent sheets of clay.

Serrated Rib: A sharp tool used for shaping pottery.

Slip: A water and clay mixture is employed in ceramics for a number of tasks.

Slurry: A thick mixture of clay and water.

Spout: A cylindrical aperture that enables fluids to be discharged from a container.

Underglaze: Ornamentation added to bisque pottery and coated with a layer of glaze

Vitrify: To transform into a glass or a glass-like material, usually by heat.

Wedging: Preparing the clay for use manually.

REFERENCES

Admin. (2020, December 8). What happens to clay as it dries and gets fired? –
Quick-Advice.com. Yourquickadvice.com. https://yourquickadvice.com/what-
happens-to-clay-as-it-dries-and-gets-fired/

Admin. (2021, January 21). What is leather-hard clay good for? – Sage-Answer.
Sage-Answer.com. https://sage-answer.com/what-is-leather-hard-clay-good-for/

Admin. (2020, July 3). What are Food-Safe Pottery Glazes? Spinning Pots.
https://spinningpots.com/what-are-food-safe-pottery-glazes/#How_-
Does_Crazing_of_Glazes_Affect_the_Food-Safety

Admin. (2022, January 16). 10 Must-Know Beautiful Pottery Glaze Techniques.
Spinning Pots. https://spinningpots.com/10-must-know-beautiful-pottery-glaze-
techniques/

Arzt, K. (2023, May 5). How To Make Pottery At Home: Materials, Equipment, &
Steps. The Crucible. https://www.thecrucible.org/guides/ceramics/pottery/

Beth Peterson. (2020, January 19). What Is Bone Dry Pottery? - Definition. The
Spruce Crafts. https://www.thesprucecrafts.com/bone-dry-2745995

Big Ceramic Store. (2023, May 5). How to Attach Clay Parts. BigCeramicStore.-
com. https://bigceramicstore.com/pages/info-ceramics-tips-tip2_attach_clay_-
parts.html

Big Ceramic Store. (2023b, May 10). Cracking, Crazing, Shivering and Dunting.
BigCeramicStore.com. https://bigceramicstore.com/pages/info-ceramics-tips-
tip40_cracking_crazing_shivering_dunting

Blewis. (2022, May 18). Air Dry Clay Embellishments. The Shabby Tree.
https://theshabbytree.com/air-dry-clay-embellishments/

Bloomfield, L. (2022, November 28). Firing Clay: The Lowdown on the Ceramic
Firing Process. Default. https://ceramicartsnetwork.org/daily/article/Firing-
Clay-The-Lowdown-on-the-Ceramic-Firing-Process

Brown, J. (2021, July 27). What happens to clay during the firing process? – Knowl-
edgeBurrow.com. Knowledgeburrow.com. https://knowledgeburrow.com/what-
happens-to-clay-during-the-firing-process/

Ceramics, S. (2023, May 5). How To Dry Pottery Clay: Process, Tips and Techniques. Soul Ceramics. https://www.soulceramics.com/pages/how-to-dry-
pottery

Ceramike. (2022, August 1). 12 Techniques For Hand Building Clay And Coil
Pottery. Ceramike. https://ceramike.com/techniques-for-hand-building-clay-
and-coil-pottery/

Chong, A. (2022, July 28). Does Clay Shrink After Firing? Terra & Ember.
https://terraandember.com/blogs/news/does-clay-shrink-after-firing

Corral, A. (2016, August 26). 5 Ceramic Techniques You Need to Know. Artsy.
https://www.artsy.net/article/artsy-editorial-5-ceramic-techniques-you-need-to-
know

Country Love Arts. (2021). Glaze Shivering Off Pottery | Country Love Crafts.
Personal Impressions. https://www.countrylovecrafts.com/glaze-shivering-off-
pottery

D'Souza, S. (2019, December 8). How to Use a Press Mold to Make Pottery. The

Spruce Crafts. https://www.thesprucecrafts.com/using-press-mold-tips-and-tricks-4091260

Davis, S. (2019). Ceramics | Office of Environmental Health and Safety. Princeton.edu. https://ehs.princeton.edu/health-safety-the-campus-community/art-theater-safety/art-safety/ceramics

Diamond Core Tools. (2021, November 19). Methods and Techniques for Firing Pottery. DiamondCore Tools. https://diamondcoretools.com/blogs/resources/firing-pottery

Erin. (2022, May 2). 8 Easy Clay Pinch Pot Ideas For Beginners. Crafty Art Ideas. https://craftyartideas.com/clay-pinch-pot-ideas/

Fern, J. (2021, October 26). Slab Pottery 101: A Handbuilding Technique. Wheel & Clay. https://wheelandclay.com/blog/slab-pottery/

Fern, K. (2022a, April 22). Handbuilding Pottery: A Complete Guide. Wheel & Clay. https://wheelandclay.com/blog/handbuilding-pottery/

Fern, K. (2022b, May 3). Coiling Pottery 101: A Handbuilding Technique. Wheel & Clay. https://wheelandclay.com/blog/coiling-pottery/

Flyschool. (2023a, May 5). The Two Rules Of Joining Clay | flyeschool.com. Flyeschool.com. http://flyeschool.com/content/two-rules-joining-clay

Flyschool. (2023b, May 5). Working With Leather Hard Clay Slabs | flyeschool.com. Flyeschool.com. http://flyeschool.com/content/working-leather-hard-clay-slabs

Greefhorst, R. (2020, June 27). 10 essentials for in your pottery studio. Studio Bloei. https://www.studiobloei.nl/blogs/news/10-essentials-for-in-your-pottery-studio

Hansen, T. (2023a). Glaze Blisters. Digitalfire.com. https://digitalfire.com/trouble/glaze+blisters

Hansen, T. (2023b). Glaze Crawling. Digitalfire.com. https://digitalfire.com/trouble/glaze+crawling

Hopper, R. (2022, September 5). How to Correct Five Common Ceramic Glaze Defects. Default. https://ceramicartsnetwork.org/daily/article/how-to-correct-five-common-ceramic-glaze-defects/

https://www.facebook.com/thespruceofficial. (2019). What Supplies Do You Need to Get Started as a Potter? The Spruce Crafts. https://www.thesprucecrafts.com/survey-of-basic-pottery-tools-2746328

Kaplan, J. (2023, January 9). Recycling Clay: Tips for Recycling Clay by Hand. Default. https://ceramicartsnetwork.org/daily/article/Recycling-Clay-Tips-for-Collecting-Storing-Reclaiming-and-Reprocessing-Your-Clay-Scraps

Lesley. (2020a, January 5). 7 Pottery Firing Methods Commonly Used - With Images. Pottery Tips by the Pottery Wheel. https://thepotterywheel.com/firing-clay/

Lesley. (2020b, January 13). 8 Reasons Pottery Clay Cracks When Drying - 11 Solutions. Pottery Tips by the Pottery Wheel. https://thepotterywheel.com/why-pottery-clay-cracks/

Lesley. (2020c, January 14). What is Bone Dry Clay? And How To Tell If Clay is Bone Dry. Pottery Tips by the Pottery Wheel. https://thepotterywheel.com/bone-dry-clay/

Lesley. (2020d, June 9). 8 Ways to Fix Handles that Crack on Mugs as Clay Dries. Pottery Tips by the Pottery Wheel. https://thepotterywheel.com/handles-that-crack-on-mugs/

Lesley. (2020e, August 14). Best Clay for Handbuilding – Tips on Choosing Pottery Clay. Pottery Tips by the Pottery Wheel. https://thepotterywheel.com/best-clay-for-handbuilding-pottery/

Lesley. (2020f, September 6). How to Make Coil Pots – 5 Great Coil Pottery Techniques. Pottery Tips by the Pottery Wheel. https://thepotterywheel.com/how-to-make-coil-pots/

Lesley. (2022, March 1). Decorating Pottery - 21 Great Ways to Decorate Clay. Pottery Tips by the Pottery Wheel. https://thepotterywheel.com/decorating-pottery/#pottery-decorating-technique-4-decorating-slip

Marie. (2018, April 30). How Long Pottery Should Dry Before Firing. Pottery Crafters. https://potterycrafters.com/how-long-pottery-should-dry-before-firing/

Marie. (2019a, January 31). The 7 Stages of Clay - And a Forgotten Number 8. Pottery Crafters. https://potterycrafters.com/the-7-stages-of-clay/

Marie. (2019b, March 23). Choosing Your Pottery Clay - Best Pottery Clay For Beginners -. Pottery Crafters. https://potterycrafters.com/best-pottery-clay-for-beginners/

Marie. (2019c, May 5). Recycle Bone Dry Clay In 6 Easy Steps - With A Guided Video - Pottery Crafters. Pottery Crafters. https://potterycrafters.com/recycle-clay/

Marie. (2019d, August 31). How To Wedge Clay A Beginner's Guide With A Step By Step Video - Pottery Crafters. Potters Crafters. https://potterycrafters.com/wedging-clay/

Marie. (2021a, January 7). Do You Glaze Pottery Before Or After Firing - Pottery Crafters. Potter Crafters. https://potterycrafters.com/do-you-glaze-pottery-before-or-after-firing/

Marie. (2021b, September 13). What Causes Pinholes In Pottery Glaze And How To Prevent Them - Pottery Crafters. Pottery Crafters. https://potterycrafters.com/what-causes-pinholes-in-pottery-glaze/

McLeod, S. (2022, November 29). The Air Bubble Myth. Sue McLeod Ceramics. https://suemcleodceramics.com/the-myth-of-air-bubbles/

Mikaelsen, M. (2019, February 18). Tips and Tricks for Using a Press Mould | VannessStudios.com. Adam Bright Pottery. https://adambrighttreeservice.com/tips-and-tricks-for-using-a-press-mould/

Naples, L. (2023, May 5). Five Expert Tips for Working with Soft Slabs. Default. https://ceramicartsnetwork.org/daily/article/5-Expert-Tips-for-Working-with-Soft-Slabs

Peterson, B. (2018, September 8). Using Slabs and Molds for Pottery. The Spruce Crafts. https://www.thesprucecrafts.com/slumping-and-draping-slabs-2746178

Peterson, B. (2019a, October 7). Understanding and Making Greenware Pottery. The Spruce Crafts. https://www.thesprucecrafts.com/greenware-what-it-means-2746003

Peterson, B. (2019b, October 28). What is Leather-hard Pottery? The Spruce Crafts. https://www.thesprucecrafts.com/leather-hard-2746007

Peterson, B. (2020a, May 13). How to Dry Your Clay Objects Right Before Firing. The Spruce Crafts. https://www.thesprucecrafts.com/drying-pottery-and-clay-objects-2746236

Peterson, B. (2020b, June 15). 8 Steps to Hand Build a Basic Slab Pot. The Spruce Crafts. https://www.thesprucecrafts.com/make-a-basic-slab-pot-2746207

Peterson, B. (2020c, August 9). What Makes Slab Pots Unique? The Spruce Crafts. https://www.thesprucecrafts.com/slab-ceramics-pots-101-2746177

Pottery, L. (2023a, May 5). Custom-made Ceramic Art | Pottery, China, Sculpture and Kintsugi Repair and Restoration. Www.lakesidepottery.com.

https://lakesidepottery.com/HTML%20Text/Tips/A%20pottery%20glossary.htm

Pottery, L. (2023b, May 5). Custom-made Ceramic Art | Pottery, China, Sculpture and Kintsugi Repair and Restoration. Www.lakesidepottery.com. https://www.lakesidepottery.com/HTML%20Text/Tips/Shivering.html

Process. (2019, August 25). The secrets and lies of creating your own glazes. Kara Leigh Ford Ceramics. https://karaleighfordceramics.com/shed-diaries/2019/8/25/a-note-on-making-your-own-glazes

Schukei, A. (2019, July 29). 4 Essential Things You Need to Know About Clay. The Art of Education University. https://theartofeducation.edu/2019/07/4-essential-things-you-need-to-know-about-clay/

Scott, S. (2023, January 11). The Clay Drying Process - Helpful Hints for Drying Pottery Evenly. Default. https://ceramicartsnetwork.org/daily/article/Protecting-Your-Pottery-and-Ceramic-Sculpture-Hints-for-Even-Drying

Spinning Pots. (2020, December 25). Slab Pottery Building Basics. Spinning Pots. https://spinningpots.com/slab-pottery-building-basics/

Terpstra, K. (2022, August 31). How to Make a Coil Pot: Using Flat Coils to Construct Large Jars. Default. https://ceramicartsnetwork.org/daily/article/How-to-Make-a-Coil-Pot-Using-Flat-Coils-to-Construct-Large-Jars

Thoresen, P. (2023, May 5). Tips for Forming the Best Ceramic Coils. Default. https://ceramicartsnetwork.org/daily/article/Tips-for-Forming-the-Best-Ceramic-Coils

Tomlinson, K. (2019, November 14). The 6 different stages of clay. Oxford Clay Handmade Ceramics. https://www.oxfordclay.co.uk/blog-1/blog-post-title-four-de9r7-9yzl3

Tomorrow's World Today. (2018, August 1). A Brief History of Pottery. TOMORROW'S WORLD TODAY®. https://www.tomorrowsworldtoday.com/2018/08/01/a-brief-history-of-pottery/

We Teach Me. (2022, December 19). How to Make a Pinch Pot: DIY Pinch Pot Ideas. WeTeachMe. https://weteachme.com/blog/articles/505-how-to-make-a-pinch-pot-diy-pinch-pot-ideas

Willis, E. S. (2023, March 20). Pinch Pot Technique - How to Make a Pinched Pitcher. Default. https://ceramicartsnetwork.org/daily/article/Pinched-Pitchers-A-Fundamental-Pottery-Technique-with-Gorgeous-Results

Wytse. (2022, November 11). 11 Easy Coil Pot Ideas Every Beginner Must Try – The Beginning Artist. Www.thebeginningartist.com. https://www.thebeginningartist.com/coil-pottery-ideas/

Wytse. (2023, March 10). 10 Easy Slab Pottery Ideas & Projects For Beginners – The Beginning Artist. Www.thebeginningartist.com. https://www.thebeginningartist.com/slab-pottery-ideas/

IMAGE REFERENCES

Brenkee. (2017, October 12). *Wind Chime Tree Sun - Free photo on Pixabay*. Pixabay. https://pixabay.com/photos/wind-chime-tree-sun-moon-clay-2819726/

Ch, A. (2022, April 21). *Painted ceramic plates. Free Stock Photo*. Pexels. https://www.pexels.com/photo/painted-ceramic-plates-11889255/

Couple, C. of . (2021, March 29). *A man holding a stick pointing to the clay ball. Free Stock Photo*. Pexels. https://www.pexels.com/photo/a-man-holding-a-stick-pointing-to-the-clay-ball-7302492/

Furkanfdemir. (2020, December 19). *Set of various ceramic pots on shelves in workshop · Free Stock Photo*. Pexels. https://www.pexels.com/photo/set-of-various-ceramic-pots-on-shelves-in-workshop-6229521/

Goodfreephotos_Com. (2014, May 11). *Jug Bellarmine Relics - Free photo on Pixabay*. Pixabay. https://pixabay.com/photos/jug-bellarmine-relics-old-ancient-347327/

Gromov, D. (2023, February 13). *Pottery on Clay Shelf · Free Stock Photo*. Pexels. https://www.pexels.com/photo/pottery-on-clay-shelf-15535542/

Hans. (2013a January 3). *Amphora Vases Pottery - Free photo on Pixabay*. Pixabay. https://pixabay.com/photos/amphora-vases-pottery-stairs-64978/

Hans. (2013b, December 30). *Lantern Volume Ceramic - Free photo on Pixabay*. Pixabay. https://pixabay.com/photos/lantern-volume-ceramic-moon-stars-232063/

Lisabahamas. (2014, June 6). *Mug Coffee Tea - Free photo on Pixabay*. Pixabay. https://pixabay.com/photos/mug-coffee-tea-coral-blue-carved-363146/

NoName. (2019, September 10). *Clay Pots Jugs - Free photo on Pixabay*. Pixabay. https://pixabay.com/photos/clay-pots-jugs-pots-pottery-4465357/

PDPics. (2013, July 24). *Plate Brown Pot - Free photo on Pixabay*. Pixabay. https://pixabay.com/photos/plate-brown-pot-clay-ceramic-166504/

Pexels. (2021, February 3). *Crack on a Clay Sculpture · Free Stock Photo*. https://www.pexels.com/photo/crack-on-a-clay-sculpture-6693593/

Photosforyou. (2018, March 1). *Pottery Art Ceramic - Free photo on Pixabay*. Pixabay. https://pixabay.com/photos/pottery-art-ceramic-handmade-3188621/

Prachuk, O. (2023, February 5). *A person doing pottery. Free Stock Photo*. Pexels. https://www.pexels.com/photo/a-person-doing-pottery-15440830/

Rspata. (2013, August 3). *Bowl Pottery Ceramic - Free photo on Pixabay*. Pixabay. https://pixabay.com/photos/bowl-pottery-ceramic-glass-rustic-169435/

Shuraeva, A. (2020, October 22). *Person Painting on Wet Clay Plate · Free Stock Photo*. Pexels. https://www.pexels.com/photo/person-painting-on-wet-clay-plate-5566959/

Studio, C. (2021b, February 3). *People doing pottery. Free Stock Photo*. Pexels. https://www.pexels.com/photo/people-doing-pottery-6694308/

Vinh, Q. N. (2019a, April 22). *Person molding brown clay. Free Stock Photo*. Pexels. https://www.pexels.com/photo/person-molding-brown-clay-2162943/

Vinh, Q. N. (2019b, April 23). *Woman making clay pot. Free Stock Photo*. Pexels. https://www.pexels.com/photo/woman-making-clay-pot-2166456/

Viviane. (2018, October 30). *Crafts Pottery Hand - Free photo on Pixabay*. Pixabay. https://pixabay.com/photos/crafts-pottery-hand-clay-decor-3778267/

ALSO BY CHLOE BECKER:

ROUTINE ESSENTIALS FOR THE MODERN POTTER

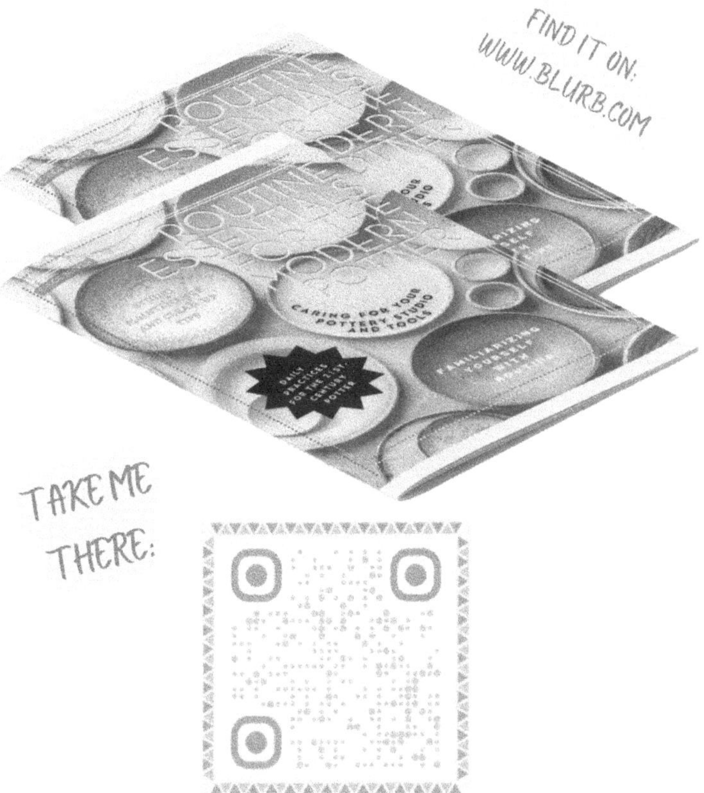

Routine Essentials for the Modern Potter is our potter's checklist. This guide will encourage you to step into your pottery studio confidently, being equipped with valuable insights and all the essential tools to help you maintain your creative space. Get your copy today.